BARBARA BAYNTON

Penne-Hackforth-Jones is an actress and journalist who is interested in Australian literary history and biography. She spent many years researching Barbara Baynton's life and writing in both Australia and the UK.

BARBARA BAYNTON

Between Two Worlds

Penne Hackforth-Jones

Melbourne University Press

First published 1989 by Penguin Books Australia

Published by Melbourne University Press, 1995

Cover designed by Mark Davis
Printed in Malaysia by SRM Production Services Sdn. Bhd. for
Melbourne University Press, Carlton, Victoria 3053

National Library of Australia Cataloguing-in-Publication entry
Hackforth-Jones, Penne.
    Barbara Baynton, between two worlds.
    ISBN 0 522 84694 7 (pbk)
    1. Baynton, Barbara, 1857-1929 - Biography. 2. Authors,
    Australian - Biography. 3. Women authors, Australian -
    Biography. I. Title.
A823.2

For my family

Preface

By the time I started to research Barbara Baynton's life she had been dead for over fifty years. It seemed then that the number of adults who had known her in her lifetime was growing smaller and if I wanted to recreate a complete picture of the woman I had to do it quickly. Barbara Baynton left no diary and very few letters. Her articles and essays, poetry and interviews are the only evidence of her life and character apart from her three published books. Because of this, information from her friends and relatives forms the backbone of this biography.

My purpose in writing about Barbara Baynton was, to a large extent, personal – an attempt to demystify an impossibly overbearing antecedent and to reconcile the two portraits I had of her: one, a battling young girl from outback New South Wales; and the other, and much more familiar, dowager from London.

In the early parts of the book – the immigration of her parents and Barbara Baynton's childhood – I have bridged gaps between known facts with the suggestions I found in her literary work.

Many people have helped me in preparing this biography. I am indebted to Karen Frater for her assistance and access to her family research. Mrs Nancy Gray, of the Scone Historical Society, guided my early research into the Lawrence family and gave me her valuable time and advice. Her work illuminated many events of Barbara's childhood and adolescence. Martha Campbell, of the *Australian Dictionary of Biography,* kindly made her research notes and the material on the entry for Barbara Baynton available to me.

I am grateful to the Jamieson family for their continued assistance with the chapters concerning the Fraters. Douglas Jamieson's family research into the early life at Merrylong provided proof for the theory that Barbara's work was deeply autobiographical.

For information regarding the life of Sarah Glover and Alex Frater, I would like to thank the children and grandchildren of that marriage, in particular Penelope Ranger, whose insights into her mother's life provided the essence of this portion of the biography. Don and Ken Frater gave me frank impressions of their mother's marriage to Barbara Baynton's first husband.

Mrs Lily Frater, wife of Alec Frater, and her family have given me their time and assistance throughout the writing and research period. I am extremely grateful to her daughters, Barbara Wilson, Alexandra Brigden and Joan Taylor, for their trust and co-operation.

I am indebted to F. R. Hocking and W. G. Millard for reminiscences of their experience in the First World War.

I am particularly grateful to Phillipa Poole for her kindness in allowing me to publish the letter her grandmother, Ethel Turner, sent to Barbara Baynton, and to the Law Book Company of Australia for allowing me access to their company records.

I would like to thank John Ferguson for his initial encouragement and introduction to Brian Johns, whose enthusiasm and concern for this project was a constant source of inspiration. I would also like to thank Rose Creswell for believing Brian Johns.

The staff of the National Library of Australia, the Mitchell Library at the State Library of New South Wales, the Fryer Memorial Library of Australian Literature at the University of Queensland, the State Library of South Australia, and the Woollahra Library in New South Wales gave me continued assistance throughout this project.

My thanks to Meryl Potter, my editor, whose understanding and thoughtfulness helped to shape this biography into a cohesive form.

The support I have received from my family has made this book possible, in particular from my parents: my mother for memories of her parents and grandmother, my father for his interest and encouragement; and my uncle, H. B. Gullett, for his knowledge of Barbara and the time.

One

Courage is your inheritance; your forebears possessed it, or they never would have sailed far away to that great and unknown country. [1]

That great unknown country lay 12,000 miles and a hazardous four months journey away for John Lawrence and his wife, Elizabeth Ewart, of Londonderry, Ireland. His wife was leaving 'father and mother, and sister and brother and friends, to face the great unknown'[2] in the belief that they would be able to build a future for themselves better than the one they faced in Ireland. At least there was hope, and that's why they had come; otherwise it was years of back-breaking work for him and domestic drudgery for her.

John Lawrence was a farm labourer with some knowledge of carpentry and he wanted to settle where the timber was good. Other Lawrences had gone before him and there were reports of cedar to be had near the Hunter River, north of Sydney, their destination. He had found himself a good match. Elizabeth was young and devoted to him, capable and domestic. At first the journey had been exciting and exhilarating for her: the marriage, the feeling of adventure, boarding the ship with her new husband and the great horizon they were slowly making their way toward. Later the horrible realization of the distance and finality of it all made her sick and silent. Even when the weather was good she stayed inside and read the Bible her mother had given her. It was familiar and calmed her. Reading it had always been a chore, but now the words took on new meaning and she clung to the images. But John was stronger and happier the further they sailed. He went out and about among the passengers, finding out what they knew of the colony, where they were heading once they arrived, what they intended to do. He had heard there was little stone in the Hunter region, which meant the wood he cut and worked would be in great demand for housing.

Their ship, the *Royal Consort*, arrived in Port Jackson on 4 November 1840. It was beautiful weather – fine and clear. All crowded on deck to watch the New Land as it spread itself before them:

old men with grey hairs and faltering steps, young girls, pale from factory or garret, countrymen in small frocks, lean faced artisans, mothers with infants in arms, stout serving girls ... two or three newly married couples ... some were trying to look unconcerned and even rather jolly, as if they knew all about it, and it was a mere nothing to them; others got up a little careless whistling, and put questions to the pilot in an imitation gruff voice.[3]

Elizabeth stared blankly into the alien corn.

The Lawrences found themselves temporary lodgings and started to plan their journey north. Most settlers rode or travelled in groups on bullock drays over the Blue Mountains, across the Hawkesbury and Colo Rivers, and through a little place called Putty to Singleton. From there they followed the Hunter upstream toward the Ranges. It was coming on to midsummer; the trip would be hot and dusty.[4]

It was said that New South Wales was neither 'Elysium nor Pandemonium', but for Elizabeth it was both. The views in the mountains had sometimes taken her breath away. She had never seen such trees or ferns, or imagined the sort of wildness she was now confronted with. The birds that darted about the bush were more brightly coloured than she would have thought possible, and she caught flashes of them as they rose, startled, in a cackling cloud that twisted in and out of itself and blew away into the air. In the early morning, strange warbling noises gossiped and chattered, while late in the afternoon as the travellers rested they heard a laugh that grew and became raucous. They left the comforting cool of the mountains and plunged into the baking plains, creaking and jolting and wishing for shade. Now they heard a bird cry that dwindled into a long slow sigh. The driver told tales of terrible hardships and strange native ways with a quiet assurance. He scared the wits out of them.

John did not enjoy the trip. He had come this far to make his way and now he heard there were signs of a depression. He was only twenty-two and good enough at what he did, but no expert. He applied for a permit to cut cedar near Murrurundi as soon as they arrived, and they settled in Scone, a small town at the foot of the Liverpool Ranges, where they lived in a rough house close to the flood-prone creek that fed the town. John was away felling timber for days at a time and came back tired, wanting only food and rest. Elizabeth hated being alone and told him of her fears, but he laughed. She was safe enough – no one would come.

Had it not been such exhausting work she would have enjoyed making the house neat and attractive, but it was so hard to provide even the basics that she was always tired and took little pleasure in it. She found the uneven wooden floor almost impossible to clean and the soap she made herself dried to a rock-like consistency so hard she had to pare it into fine shavings before it would dissolve. Washing alone took all her strength – setting the fire under the copper, tending it, sorting and steeping the clothes and hanging them.[5] Some women had to haul the firewood out of the forest in logs when their men were away. They were old at forty and considered themselves so.

The Lawrences had arrived in the height of summer and, added to the continual war against the buzzing horrors that hovered around anything edible, the hot nights were alive with mosquitoes. Fresh food was hard to find at any price because of the uncertain rainfall. Elizabeth worked day and night and slowly a strong sense of order developed.

Sometimes she went out with John to help, but the pleasure she took in his company was counterbalanced by a vague feeling of unrest. She pitied the trees as they were separated from their own, imagining they had voices and softly spoke to each other in the wind, sighing as they fell.

In 1843, two years after the Lawrences had settled in Scone, Elizabeth gave birth to her first child, a daughter. She was a healthy baby and her mother loved her. They called her Elizabeth, and when her mother raised a murmur about a son the midwife scoffed back her worries with 'What do you want to do with a brat of a boy?', and she accepted that.

Now that his family had grown, John was forced to seek a more substantial income. The depression had deepened and while cedar was cheap to cut, it was as cheap to sell, and he had no particular skills to render it into anything fine. He became a coffin-maker, and his tappings and sawings could be heard along the street at night, blending with the town's other night noises.

To the small population of Scone, the reminders of their mortality were never far away. In the elaborate ritual of death, strange obsessions seemed to comfort rather than repel. Pennies placed on the eyes of the dead were kept in jars and shown to children as souvenirs of the departed, and the tolling bell brought the town to a standstill as they counted the chimes: 'one for a child, two for a woman, three for a man ... four for thee?' They muttered and bless me'd and moved on.[6]

Elizabeth had another daughter, Sarah, in 1846, and two years later the first son, John. There was barely enough time to recover before another was on the way. She read more of the Bible, determined her children would never forget their heritage and the battles their ancestors had fought to protect their religion. Many of their neighbours were Irish and the bitterness with which they set up their respective churches split the little township from the beginning. Elizabeth was a Protestant whose ancestors had 'fought and bled and DIED on the walls of Derry' and Elizabeth would pass on that know-ledge. It was a link with the past and links were important now.[7]

As the family grew, there evolved an elaborate system of clothing them all. The eldest had the newest clothes, a little too large so they would last, and when these were outgrown they flowed on to the next child. When the clothes finally fell apart, they were cut up and pieced together and started back at the top again, sewn into little 'pied piper' coats and dresses, which gave the children a colourful and wild appearance.

By 1845 the depression was easing. A pecking order had

developed in the town. On Sunday it was important to turn up at church in something resembling a best dress and good hat and gloves. Elizabeth tried hard with the children, who nevertheless looked like a band of gypsies with their shabby, uneven clothes.

Two years after the birth of her first son she had her second, David, and a third, Robert, in 1852. The two girls were by then eight and six, old enough to help around the house and look after the babies. The boys would help their father in his trade and be apprenticed out later.

In 1855 the Lawrences had another daughter, Mary Ann, and two years later a fourth, Barbara. Elizabeth was now thirty-seven, and it seemed wise to have the assistance of Dr Goodwin, in his own words the best, 'the most scientific and sober, skilful and temperate man in the whole district of Scone'. He was a Presbyterian 'by birth, title and principle', cantankerous but kind-hearted, a personality in the town who much preferred the gratitude of his poorer clients to the fat fees of the richer 'swindling scoundrels' and 'gilded wretches' of local settlers.[8]

Three years later Elizabeth had her last child, a boy named James, but this time there was no Dr Goodwin to attend her, only the local midwife, Mrs Hatherall.[9] When John Lawrence registered the child, he claimed the little boy as his own, but gave as the child's surname his mother's maiden name of Ewart, and described him as 'illegitimate'. There were no witnesses to the birth, and shortly afterwards John Lawrence left for Murrurundi, a small town at the foot of the Liverpool Ranges.

Later her grand-daughter Penelope would remember Elizabeth Lawrence as gloomy and very religious. In old age she stayed with her daughter Barbara in Sydney where, haunted perhaps by the burden of some great sin, she regularly attended church alone.

The year James was born was her fortieth. She was old and considered herself so.

Two

The illegitimacy of the last child of the Lawrences has always been a puzzle, but it seems likely that all the Lawrence children were illegitimate. A certificate registered in Murrurundi in 1862, two years after James was born, records the marriage of Elizabeth Lawrence, widow, and Robert John Lawrence, bachelor. The ceremony between the two people with identical surnames took place in a private house, and few details of the Lawrences' births or origins were entered in the register.

In later years, Barbara claimed that her father was in fact Robert Kilpatrick, a Bengal Lancer, who had met her mother on board the ship coming out to Australia. It seems she glamourized a story that was in part true. Robert Kilpatrick, a twenty-year-old carpenter from the same county in Ireland as the Lawrences, had arrived in Sydney some months before them.[1] The most likely explanation is that Elizabeth left her husband, a farm labourer, after their arrival in Sydney. Because Elizabeth was unable to divorce, Kilpatrick seems to have taken John Lawrence's name, and the couple moved to Scone, where they lived as man and wife. But by the time James was born, the secret was out, and Elizabeth could no longer pose as a married woman. In 1862, probably because of the death of her husband, they were able to marry. By then Robert Kilpatrick, still living under the name of John Lawrence, had moved to Murrurundi, a growing town the next stop along the railway line, and he took the elder boys with him, to begin work as apprentices.

Elizabeth became very conscious of her precarious standing in the community and behaved from then on with great propriety. She took care to appear regularly in church, and to dress the children as well as possible for it. The younger ones played outside, watching the animals and insect life.

In the early 1860s, when John was old enough to join his father, he went to Murrurundi, leaving David as head of the house and the two elder girls to help their mother with the smaller children. They were pretty and domestic. Elizabeth especially was extremely good with the children and much preferred domesticity to any outside interests. Like her mother, she had never learnt even the rudiments of spelling or writing and was looking about now for a husband.[2]

Before John had left, one of the girls had gone out with a local boy and come home to find her father full of questions: 'Who was it? Oh, O'Neill was it? Catholic would he be? Right then. There'll be no more of him!' There were storms of tears and recriminations, but that was that. No Catholic would marry into the house, and there was an end to it. To add to the family's own Protestant fervour, the hostility between the two churches was fanned by constant skirmishes within the town. The children carried on the tradition with great glee, hurling stones at the opposition, jeering and catcalling and making up names. But as they grew, the clean divisions became awkward to maintain and steps were made toward conciliation.[3]

Among the Lawrence children David was clever with the smaller ones, his ingenuity and kindness making him a favourite. One day, taking Barbara and James out for a walk, he had gone too far, and they had refused to walk back and demanded to be carried. 'Knocked up are you; then you must ride home' – and he made them little stick horses which they beat into a lather in the race to get home, forgetting their tiredness completely.[4] They enjoyed having him there and he became the father figure they all missed.

In 1865 John returned to Scone to go to the funeral of an old friend; shortly after David joined him, followed by Robert. That same year young Elizabeth married, and Mrs Lawrence was left with a much smaller family to look after. Barbara was not much inclined to help around the house but Mary Ann was more like the other girls and was content with little things, 'always smiling and happy as long as her canary sang and her handiwork sold, darning the holes in the overworn carpet, thrilling with enthusiasm over her success as a stallholder in a church bazaar, sleepless the night before a Sunday School picnic!'[5] Barbara, as the youngest girl, had always had to fight for herself, and she was strong-willed and sharp-witted enough to win most times. She was inquisitive and would have enjoyed outside life much more had her shortsightedness not made it a terrifying experience. Added to this, the dust and flies had given her Sandy Blight and weakened her eyes even more. It terrified her to be suddenly lost and to have to identify objects close to hand before stumbling on to the next.[6] It drew her world close around her and made her introspective, the mind's eye seeing what the other would not. She learnt to read very quickly, holding the book inches from her face. Yet she hated staying indoors; the little house depressed her and she wanted to be off where the colours were bright and things were interesting. The docile discipline of her elder sisters enraged and then amused her, and she laughed and imitated them so accurately that the confused victim found herself laughing too, and lost the battle before she even started. When anyone commented on this youngest and strangest Lawrence girl, the good-natured sisters would shrug and say, 'it's just Barbara's way'.[7]

As her younger brother, James, grew she had a companion to go roaming with and they could escape into the perpetually dry crackling grasses and the hot air humming with insects. If they went far enough into the hills they could find huge goannas to chase, frilled-neck lizards with blue tongues, possums, bandicoots and wallabies. And snakes. Death adders sunned themselves on warm flat rocks, bush rats and mice scuttled about. In the hills galahs and cockatoos flew screaming, and their colour and vivacity contrasted wildly with the black cunning of the crows clustering together in the tree tops.

Nearer to home, Fig Tree Gully was full of frogs and toads croaking 'quoit roit', kingfishers built nests, and sometimes, when there was water enough, small flocks of ibis came. Scented native violets grew at the edges of the rocks, and further up in the hills greenhood orchids. There was also a wilder and more cruel side: in the poor seasons the eagles ripped the kidneys from fallen sheep and even the beautiful call of the butcher bird could not disguise its savagery with the smaller birds it killed and hung about the bush to dry.[8]

Barbara came home and told tales of her adventures, spiking the boring bits with her imagination and making use of her already good vocabulary to keep her audience amused. Her mother acknowledged the exaggeration resignedly: it was 'Barbara's way'.

They understood each other, these two. The child was difficult and rebellious, but even at her most terrified was quickly calmed when mother placed her hands over the child's head and gravely smiled. The little girl had small fine hands, which Elizabeth took in hers to recite her favourite prayer, 'Bless, pardon, protect and guide, strengthen and comfort.'[9]

A favourite place for Barbara and James was 'Chinamen's gardens' on the outskirts of town, where they could watch the Chinese cultivate their vegetables, the only vivid splash of green for miles around. They had to cross Fig Tree Gully to get to the gardens, over a plank footway to the fence, where they waited, staring through the bars at the ceaseless activity. There was a delicious mixture of excitement and terror. By every Chinaman's side hung a large knife for cutting cabbages – but really it was for cutting heads off, everyone knew that. The scurry and hurry as the Chinamen moved along the rows, watering the plants from large tins suspended across their backs, the rhythmic trot, all added to the exotic vision.[10]

On Saturdays, when the Chinese market gardeners carried their vegetables in a dray around the town, the children would follow it and hitch a ride on top. Scrubbed carrots and other vegetables were waiting for them as treats, and if times were hard and there were children to feed, more would change hands than had been paid for. The little cart with its burden of produce fed the town that had never grown its own, and while Ireland provided basic meat and potatoes, China added as much variety from its cuisine as it could extract from the baked earth.

Sometimes at night a wild commotion was heard as carts were driven at full gallop through the town, carrying the newly dead to the cemetery. Wailing and keening followed the sound of horses' hooves, and the next day there would be offerings left at a new grave. Barbara went with the others to see: they found beautiful little bowls of fine china, white and

9

green, pink and yellow, with patterns of flowers and birds in clear, bright colours.

When the adventures led to accidents, there were limited remedies to cope with them. Chills were cured with a teaspoon of sugar doused in kerosene, and loose teeth were jolted out by strings tied from tooth to door, which was then slammed. Bottles of coloured water flavoured with cayenne pepper were sold as pain killers, and castor oil, in deep blue bottles, was brought out to settle troubled stomachs.

It was as well Elizabeth had someone around the house. A woman alone was marked prey for travelling salesmen and tramps. Men moving from one seasonal job to another would mark the fence of a 'soft touch' for others to follow. It was difficult to ignore the obvious threat in their eyes and the knowing way they looked at the little house, sizing up its weaknesses. Gathering strength from neighbours to resist, Elizabeth would deny them money. The small mark would then be changed and the word passed from man to man to create trouble. Chickens would be let out, the dog untied. In the morning the dog would be gone and the chickens scattered all over town, laying their eggs in other people's backyards. They were minor incidents but regular and menacing. In the end it was best to give in.

Three

In 1870 David Lawrence, Elizabeth's most dependable son and Barbara's favourite brother, married a Miss Trayhurn of Maitland. He had learned his trade as a miller in Murrurundi and his business sense and earnestness were obvious enough to the father of Miss Trayhurn, even though he was only nineteen.

In April of the following year the railway finally reached Scone. On Monday the seventeenth, the shops were shut and flags were hung in the streets as the town gathered to watch the governor's special train arrive. People came for miles to cheer the Earl of Belmore, when, to the accompaniment of Mr Prince's Volunteer Band for West Maitland, he stepped out onto the platform and declared the Great Northern Railway open to Scone.

Apart from the blessings of easy travel and the increase in business as farmers from surrounding areas flocked to make use of the new rail bulkhead, the nights were now filled with whistlings and shuntings as the train pulled in and out of the little station, picking up goods and livestock, depositing passengers.

Barbara, at fourteen, was fascinated by the trains and went to watch as the water was fed into the engine through a leather hose attached to a tank above the station, the water belching down the pipe, making it shudder and seethe like a live thing. The train tracks ran just behind the house and the noise of its comings and goings irritated her until its constant intrusions turned the train into a monster, hungry and loud.

Barbara had been to the state school but it had not been a happy experience, as she, 'weird of face, her diminutive body dressed in misfitting clothes, was from the outset a target. An unconscious smile would be styled an insolent grimace, and as such chastised; the following soberly ordered countenance was a sullenness equally punished'.[1] She had been beaten regularly as an example to the school and day by day grew accustomed to the fact that the better dressed, and therefore more prosperous, students escaped these punishments. Her longing for decent clothes and prosperity, or prosperity and decent clothes, became part of her being.

Nothing, however, could dull the appeal of the written word. Reading the weekly newspaper with its town gossip was quickly followed by a collection of books with discordant titles, ranging from *The History of Jerusalem* to *Maria Monk*, the tragic heroine of countless attempted kidnappings. Shakespeare and the Old and New Testaments were dismissed along the way on account of their inaccuracy and shabby bindings – everyone knew Leah was a girl's name.[2] *Pilgrim's Progress* had been thoroughly absorbed long before, and under its influence she had reserved an abandoned vineyard along the river for her Garden of Gethsemene. When the School of Arts opened in Scone in 1870, it provided a large collection of books – classics, romances and reference – together with a regular programme of lectures and plays. Here Barbara could read contemporary works and magazines that had the latest in poetry and serials from London, as well as articles on art and literature.[3]

On Sundays she went to church, more out of a sense of duty to her mother and a feeling for social gatherings, than reverence. Mother's God was a vengeful God, but Barbara's was a wilder spirit, more dramatic than one that could fit into the local chapel. The form – not the content – appealed to her: the 'sounding brass' and words spoken 'with the tongue of men and of angels'.

Still, it was a chance to meet people and chances were few. Occasionally the sectarian barriers were lowered and Barbara found her way to a party where she and James were the only Protestants. They dressed themselves as best they could for these occasions, borrowing tokens of splendour from the rest of the family to brighten up their appearance. The Irish in them, which led to the joyful singing of 'Fry the bobbies in a pan', also led to the formation of a strict little social pyramid up which everyone tried to scramble as fast as they could. The best of the neighbourhood could be relied on to turn up in what finery they had; a few 'kedrilles' were danced and maybe a little French was spoken. 'Parley vu frongsie, sher tray beang, jer tray beang parley vu frongsie sher tray bu parley frongsie, sher parley' brought the house down in startled amusement that a whole civilized nation could speak 'sich gatherin' gibberish'.[4] The local cobbler brought out his violin and lovingly played 'Green Grow the Rushes, O' and wept, and various children took turns at the piano. Barbara and James listened, she with her mother's purple ribbons taken from a hat and tied round the waist of her Sunday best, and James with his brother's big watch and chain.

By 1875 Barbara was of an age where a job or a marriage would have to be chosen. Several boys had taken an interest in her, but the visit of a circus to town when she was a child had set her mind on other things. After they had packed up and gone, they had left behind a vision of other places, away from the heat and flies, the daily chores and grinding sense of isolation to 'that great world beyond these hills and near the sea . . . she took from the sitting-room shelf a shell, and placing it against her ear, she listened to its sea call to her.'[5]

She was an attractive but strange girl, small-boned, with a sallow complexion and long dark hair. She looked at the available boys as a fish might look through a bowl at a large distorted vision of humanity moving silently and monstrously about. No one could compare with her brother David. When they spoke she winced. The mangled vowels and misused words became etched in her mind. Her feelings came in rushes and at odd times. She cried alone, and always felt out of step with what was expected of her. Her ability to freeze her emotions until she could release them in an ugly rush in private earned her a reputation as an actress, and for a while she seriously considered this, conjuring up an image of Kate Ashton, dancing her seven-year-old way through fiery hoops in a spangled dress, reclining at night with boxes of chocolates, doing Highland flings on the back of piebald ponies. But Barbara could barely raise a trot on the back of 'old Cushla',

and then only with James leading it.[6] She could sing – a bit –
but she needed training and there was no money. Elizabeth was
taking in washing to make ends meet and the boys were in
Murrurundi, serving their apprenticeships. One day, taunted to
the point of retaliation with all her grand ambitions, she had
flung back 'Well, if I can't be an actress I'm going to write a
book', and that seemed the most likely prospect. She needed
no school, only time and the need to tell something. Before
that, she needed a job.

Answering an advertisement for a housekeeper, she travelled
to Sydney and boarded a train for a station near Goorianawa,
in the far north-west of New South Wales. The journey was
difficult and tiring, with the train creeping along the track to
avoid the sheep, its trucks filled with thirsty cattle who inter-
mittently thudded to the floor in the blazing heat. Embers and
soot flew in through the windows unless they were kept tightly
shut, and the temperature steadily rose. The only refreshment
was a bottle of stale water, bumping along in a metal container
near the ceiling, just out of her reach.

She travelled across a barren plain, feeling sick and appre-
hensive, closing her eyes against the glare and monotony of the
view. They stopped at a siding to take on water and a bushman
got off. A woman asked where they were, and a voice from the
drover's truck called out, 'This is ther Never-Never – ther lars'
place Gord made.'[7]

At the next siding there was a cart waiting for her and
a young rouseabout announced he had come to meet a
'young piece' from Sydney. He peered at her. She was naturally
sallow with hooded eyes, and was now very pale from the
journey. She asked, '"Was it a housekeeper?" ... "Damned if
I know," he said with a snort, "but there'll be a 'ell of a
row somew'ere." '[8]

They travelled to the station through a series of gates, across
a vast plain, taking a detour via the wine shanty. The
countryside seemed more stricken with drought than the one
she had left, and the leafless plain only exacerbated the harsh
impression and made her long for some hill to rest her eyes on.

By the time they had arrived at the station her escort had
drunk himself into a muttering heap. She was eating her meal

in the dining-room when the boss arrived and she heard the rouseabout say,

'The on'y woman I see was a 'alf chow, an' she ses she's the one, an' she's in ther dinin'-room 'avin' a tuck in.'

She was too giddy to stand when the boss entered, but she turned her mournful eyes on him; and, supporting herself by the table, stood and faced him.

He kept on his hat, and she, watching, saw curiosity and surprise change into anger as he looked at her.

'What an infernal cheek *you* had to come! Who sent you?' he asked stormily.

She told him, and added that she had no intention of remaining.[9]

She spent the night in her predecessor's room, full of rouge pots and cheap scent, and in the morning was asked to 'bundle yer duds tergether quick an' lively' and 'do a get'.[10]

Travelling back in the train, going over the details of this terrible event in her mind, she vowed it would never happen again. Inexperience had led her to believe that a job as a housekeeper would mean just that. She had not meant to keep the men of the house as well.

The next advertisement she answered was for a governess for a family living at Merrylong, a property over the Liverpool Ranges on the black soil plains. The Fraters had a family of seven children, the youngest needing instruction. Barbara had no qualifications, but she could read and write, she could add, and she could imagine. It was enough. It would have to be.

Four

Alexander and Penelope Frater had settled at Merrylong after a long and stormy introduction to the colony. She was the fifth daughter of Peter and Mary Hay of Kirkcudbright, Scotland;[1] he was an orphan from Northumberland, a bull-necked shepherd with piercing brown eyes and a reputation for violence. The Hays had descended from the Earls of Kinnoull and were conscious of their ancestry. The head of their family had taken part in the uprising of 1745 and had been executed as a result.[2]

Alexander had nothing to look back on except a series of outbursts when his temper, bred through a long and lonely childhood, had got the better of him. He had killed a man, it was rumoured, in a side-show, boxing for money.[3] Dark and wilful, in a family full of girls,[4] Penelope was strongly attracted to him, but her father forbade them to marry. They ran away twice and were brought back twice. The third time the Hays resigned themselves to the inevitable, and Alexander and Penelope were married in 1850 and the next year set sail for Australia.[5]

The journey over was horrendous. A storm blew up in the Bay of Biscay and the women and children were battened down in the holds to protect them. Alexander stayed on deck, preferring that to the possibility of drowning, sealed up in the cabins below. The ship stopped in South America, and years later the Fraters would have returned and settled there if the memory of the voyage hadn't discouraged them.[6] Penelope was pregnant when they arrived in Australia in May 1851 with two shillings between them.

They took a ship to Newcastle and travelled inland to Armidale where, with winter coming on, Alexander signed for a three-year term to work sheep on Moredun Station, a huge property in a remote and desolate part of New England.[7]

In October 1851 Penelope gave birth to her first child, John.[8] She was seventeen, very homesick, and stuck in a cold and distant part of the colony. Alexander was doing well in his first job, but he broke his contract and brought his young wife and baby back across the mountains to the comparative civilization of Tamworth. Penelope and the baby John rode while Alexander walked stolidly beside them, 75 miles over unmade roads, through the cold mountain nights.[9]

Once in Tamworth, Alexander was pursued by his ex-employer, and an advertisement offering a reward appeared in the local paper. He chose to go back to Armidale to serve the rest of his indenture. Afterwards his employers were eager for him to stay on, but once free he knew he could find better jobs. By 1860 he was overseer at Trinkey, a good property, running sheep and cattle – the 'pick of the Liverpool Plains'.[10]

The Fraters by then had three children – the last, Alex,* was born in 1859. They had risen in standing enough to have the death of their second son, Peter, reported in the Maitland *Mercury* two years before.[11] He had been four years old and named after his grandfather.

Now nearing his seventies and with three of his daughters overseas, Peter Hay decided to distribute some of the family's possessions before he died. Penelope's share of plate and silver, pewter and porcelain, rugs and furniture arrived in three dray loads one day when her father, seeing a figure pumping water outside a small house, asked to be directed to the Fraters' house. He would have recognized the slim dark figure and upright carriage at once if his eyesight hadn't been so bad.

She still had a broad Scots accent and referred to Bonnie Prince Charlie as though he were her brother. Going briskly about her business she sang 'I know who I am, And I know where I'm going' as if to remind herself to keep Alexander's eye on higher and better things. With her tiny hands and feet

---

*To distinguish the three Alexander Fraters in Barbara's life, the first, her father-in-law, is always called Alexander; her husband, Alex; and her son, Alec.

she was not designed for heavy work, and she took great pride in the fact, seeing it as a sign of her aristocratic background. As soon as the children were old enough they were delegated jobs around the house, and when they could afford it Penelope gave up heavy work entirely and concentrated on her knitting.[12]

Meanwhile Alexander had calmed his temper, got on with his responsibilities as overseer at Trinkey, and gradually became an identity in the neighbourhood. When he left the district in 1882, his fellow residents described him as 'an individual of straightforward conduct with no ostentatious display in public movements but an extension of the ready and willing hand of charity to everything provocative of the public good'.[13] His work as an overseer and a manager had advanced him to the extent that by 1870 he was part owner of Merrylong, a good property on the black soil plains. He built a house with a high cool roof and long French windows and had a photograph taken of himself and the family outside on the verandah.

By then they had seven children, five boys and two girls. Alexander had increased the size of the property with each birth, keeping a horse ready saddled through Penelope's labour, to ride off into town and claim another 640 acres under the John Robertson Free Selection Act as soon as the sex and health of the child were determined.

By the time Barbara was due to arrive at Merrylong, the eldest son, John, was an easy-going and attractive boy who had begun to be interested in women – and they in him. In his early twenties he sired a daughter, Fanny, whom Penelope instantly took into the family.[14] If it was an easy solution, it would not be so with the girls, who were protected and supervised and expected to marry well. Prospective suitors were screened, and very few ever considered quite good enough, with the result that the girls were awkward and prim, with none of the wild exuberance that had brought their parents together.

By 1876 the last child, Fergus, was born and Alexander felt secure enough to indulge an expensive taste in racehorses. He built elaborate stables to house them, with china drinking troughs, brass coat-pegs and corridors of cross-hatched timber.

With Merrylong filled with china and rugs, pewter and

silver, and stables better than most people's houses, the children were the next area of improvement. Penelope had hired several Englishmen as tutors, disgraced aristocrats or younger sons of English peers, who lasted for a while, filling the children's ears with the unaccustomed sound of English spoken lovingly and well. Sooner or later, though, shocked by the sight of goannas, eyes bulging, hanging upside down by the tail while the children went calmly in to lunch, or dazed by continuous choruses of 'Little Fahrtin' Johnnie', they wandered off into town, and were never seen again.[15]

A small schoolhouse had been built at Merrylong with a bedroom at the back and a view over the plain toward the hills in the distance. The Fraters decided to hire a woman this time – less likely to abscond to the pub – and to put her in the little building, a step away from the main house.

Five

When she arrived at Merrylong in the late 1870s, Barbara must have felt a sense of relief. It was an established, well-run property, and the job genuine. The more enviable the Fraters' position became to her, the more anxiously she tried to convey to them her suitability as governess. She could teach French, English and mathematics, she said. Looking at the children, she could see it was going to be uphill all the way.

Penelope had given up on the younger children. They played outside, filthy in the mud, singing rude songs to one another and torturing little animals. When it rained, they threw cut-up sugar bags over their heads and ran around like goblins. And they had no sentimental attachment to anything: if it was stronger than you, you obeyed it; if it ran away you caught it; if it was edible you shot it. The older ones had melted down the pewter mugs from Scotland for buckshot, and the younger ones shovelled the rich dark soil into Georgian silver 'buckets' with a set of antique oyster forks.[1]

There were three Fraters to teach: Dukie, aged eleven, Lal, eight, and Mary, six, as well as Ginny and Sis Lennard from nearby. Their mother was Jane Lennard, whose reputation as midwife, or 'Rabbit Ketcher', gave her some standing. Poor, and living in a tent with three generations of Lennards, she was a proud, forceful character with prominent rabbit-like teeth, 'the last of which was always visible, without any apparent effort on her part'.[2]

Penelope was struggling to re-create as much of her old life in Scotland as she could.[3] She bought magazines from England and toured the countryside looking for furniture. She tried to establish a garden and learnt the botanical names of the local flowers. If there was a neighbour in labour she rode miles to help, but when her own time came she brought a nurse in from town.

Penelope sometimes felt as if she were struggling against an overwhelming tide. She had sent her second surviving son, Alex, to Sydney to be educated, only to have him return, unable to tolerate city life. He was her favourite son, nicknamed 'Doc' for his ability to fix anything, and an excellent horseman. Blond and gangly at seventeen he was a 'hobbledehoi, neither man nor boy'.[4]

Barbara settled herself into the small room at the back of the schoolhouse. The children were difficult to teach, resentful of being inside, uninterested in learning. The respect they had for bushcraft was not extended to academic knowledge and Barbara had no skills to show off to earn that respect. She was a bad rider and a worse 'bush scholar'. Her attitude to animals was town bred.[5] Here, every gentle thing was balanced by some horror: the lambs with their eyes torn out; the native bear looking down with its amazed and dignified stare, shot from its branch for its pelt. This sensitivity was not tolerated by the Fraters. It had no place, and, worse still, no use. Incomprehension was cause for fear and doubly so among children who, sensing a weak spot in their teacher, would capitalize on it until she had no control at all. She became strict and forceful: right or wrong, her word was law.

Barbara's attempts to impress literature on them were laughable. The one thing she had got from her schooldays was the ability to escape through books. She fought hard to get them through the alphabet, letter by letter, the sounds blending to form a whole – only to find that the end result was an appetite for penny dreadfuls alternating with a sense of total boredom.[6] The main drive of life was the outside world. Having learnt to read, her pupils stared up at her, unimpressed.

Alexander Frater continued to race horses and prosper, returning tipsily from race meetings with his four boys.[7] They were beginning to follow his example, blending liquor with their image of manliness, along with riding, shearing, shooting and gambling. The young Alex was a favourite with the children – gentle and responsive, he could read well and enjoyed it, riding regularly into town for the newspaper.[8] He began to spend more time around the schoolhouse.

His father was well aware of the effect the governess was having on his son. Hoping to embarrass her, he brought a French-speaking neighbour around, knowing Barbara had very little of the language. She shooed him away with a pretence of other and better things to do, but the children heard of the incident.[9] Still she continued to spend time with Alex, inventing elaborate mathematical problems for the children to do in her absence and marking their answers continually wrong until they lined up sticks on the floor and counted them out determinedly in front of her.

The closer she got to this young man, the more the spectre of spinsterhood receded, and her mistress, Penelope Frater, was beginning to show signs of approval. The governess was not a 'flirty, cheap woman'.[10] She could control the children, and doubtless would control her son. Alex, though charming, was lazy. He would need her.

Penelope had become quite fond of Barbara, whose love of beautiful things had made her watchful and appreciative of her employer's possessions. Penelope had given her a small piece of jewellery and been amazed at the reaction. Barbara thanked her continuously and profusely. It made a welcome change from the indifference of her own children. The vanity she had instilled into her daughters for being part of the Hay family had made them shy and tongue-tied, but Barbara had nothing to lose from such effusive compliments.[11] And Penelope was grateful to the teacher for the peace she now had. Barbara was there whenever Jane's children ran helter-skelter through the dining-room, breaking crockery and letting the fowls in, and when the parson's composure was wrecked by Jane Lennard's detailed descriptions of the rigours of childbirth. Penelope wilted, while Barbara watched. Later Barbara's precise and deadly re-enactment of the scene, Jane's every idiosyncrasy exploited, would entertain Penelope.

Stung by her treatment at Goorianawa, Barbara had arrived at Merrylong radiating correctness and propriety with every move she made. The children had thought her 'on the stuck up side',[12] but Penelope had welcomed the strong-willed, upright little woman, and with Penelope's approval came the approval of the elder Frater daughter, Elizabeth.[13] Barbara began to learn as much as she could. She copied her mistress's air of reserve and haughtiness, asked about life in Scotland, learnt a little of the history of the pieces that had been brought out, borrowed the magazines that came from England, and learnt to trim a hat. The only thing she could do in recompense was reduce Penelope's tormentors, in the form of unruly neighbours and the wild ecstatic streak in the Frater children, to bearable proportions by laughing at them. She became acutely watchful and accurate in her observation of people around her, and consequently an excellent mimic. This was her role in the family and she played it with skill and deftness. A lot depended on it.

Six

As Penelope's liking for Barbara increased, Alexander Frater's distrust of her grew. He could see his wife had begun to tire of the harsh, isolated life at Merrylong and that the governess was sympathizing with her. He had worked hard to establish the property and he wasn't going to be moved off it so easily. He resented the airs and graces Barbara gave herself, and the way she corrected his son's grammar in public. In June 1880, when Alexander discovered his son had proposed to her, all his deepest suspicions seemed confirmed. She'd been plotting and scheming and now she'd won.[1] His sense of outrage was backed up by a storm of what he considered legitimate protest at the enormous difference in their ages: Barbara was twenty-three and Alex twenty-one. He refused to give his consent and kept as many of his children away from the ceremony as he could. Taking matters firmly into her own hands, Penelope climbed into the buggy with her daughter Elizabeth and drove the young couple into Tamworth to be married in the Presbyterian church.

Once the deed was done Alexander could not allow his son to start with nothing. The pregnancy he had suspected and the birth he hoped to witness well before the regulation nine months did not appear, and so he reluctantly gave Alex a parcel of undeveloped scrubland near Coonamble, 150 miles north-west of Merrylong. To Fanny and the rest of the Frater children, it seemed that Penelope had given Barbara half the contents of Merrylong, but the young couple took off one morning with all their things packed into the back of a buggy and a couple of dairy cows trotting along behind.

Barbara was heading toward a new life of isolation and poverty. The countryside around Coonamble was scrubland, flat and monotonous, and frequently drought-stricken. In the post office directory of the time, Coonamble is described as a 'Township of 300 inhabitants on the Castlereagh river. The principal buildings are two churches and two schools.' To Barbara, it was 'dismal and drunken'.

The house they came to was probably the typical one of the time, spartan, with little more than was needed for survival. Most had a main kitchen and living area with a division down one end for the bedroom. They were built of vertical greenwood boards that shrank and warped with time, leaving irregular holes for the wind and insects to enter. The windows were usually small and over-shadowed by a corrugated iron roof that swept down in front to form a small verandah. The floor was roughly boarded. In the morning the swelling heat expanded the iron roof and at night it shrank, creaking and snapping.

The land was mostly scrub, which would need clearing and hard work to turn it into good pasture. Alex would do neither. He was content to keep a few cattle for domestic use and to hire himself out as a stockman or shearer. He built fences for livestock and tried to teach Barbara what he could of animal husbandry. She could turn the cows onto the plain during the day, he told her, and there was a creek with good feed along it for the calves. She was frightened when she tried to separate the cows from their calves and had to be forced to do it. Alex first laughed and then lost patience and swore at her, disgusted. When she finally had forced the animal to do as she wanted and came back white-faced and trembling with the stick he had given her to brandish still in her hand, she wondered if he too would run if she tried the same on him.[2]

The days went by, and slowly the shape of their lives began to form. Alex rose early, went out to feed the animals, returned home for breakfast, and spent the rest of the day smoking and reading the papers.[3] He had no intention of doing anything other than while away his time as pleasantly as he could while keeping the property in reasonable running order. He gambled at the local races and worked occasionally as a shearer, leaving before daybreak for his week at the shed. It made Barbara nervous. It was easy to see she was alone, and the nearest neighbour was a day's ride away.

She had her dog. It seemed to respond to her moods, whining when she cried and trotting briskly about in the glare of the morning, helping to herd the cattle. At night it was her only signal if a noise was anything other than normal. She had to discipline her mind never to elaborate – a creak of timber was not a groan, the quivering note to the east only a curlew. She looked round the house, checking the catches on the windows. It was hopeless. The hinge on the door was hide that could be slit in a minute with a half-sharp knife. Chairs could be stacked against the door, but that wouldn't prevent someone setting light to the house if they wanted.

When Alex returned she was overwhelmed with relief. She was alone and utterly helpless she told him, penned up here in a house only partly safe, with no rifle, no money to bargain with.

She looked forward to going to race meetings with him though, to make an occasion of something and to meet people from the area. Despite Alex's losses, it was a good outing at the races – practically anything was better than Coonamble. They made an odd couple – she slightly ashamed of his alcoholic exuberance and he embarrassed by her open courting of the gentry. Alex loved gambling and had a good eye for horses. He walked with a free and easy gait and wore a flaring silk handkerchief drawn in a sailor's knot around his neck. Years of being waited on by his sisters had given him an attitude towards women that he carried into his everyday dealings with them and seemed to give him an irresistible air of manliness.[4] While the women were absorbing this easy lolloping charm, his wife was wondering how long she could bear to watch their slim resources flow in and out of his pocket so quickly. Travelling home she often wondered if he lost deliberately to give himself a reason to return; it was like a religion with him and seemed to take the place of something greater in his life. But it offended her to see the money that could buy them essential things thrown away. They needed everything.

By June 1881 she was pregnant. The nearest doctor was a hundred miles away and by the time he'd heard of her confinement and come all that way he would be too late to deliver the child. Jane Lennard would come, but memories of her were too fresh. She put off making a decision and in November gave birth to her first baby, alone, without Alex, doctor, or witness of any kind. It was a boy and they called him Alexander after his father and grandfather.[5]

She had not made friends with the women in the area, and now she felt her aloneness keenly. To her surprise the baby gave her a sense of joy and closeness that she had never had before: he was her responsibility and his utter helplessness appealed to her. She could have asked one of her sisters to come, but she was suspicious of them. She didn't trust Alex with other women and had the distinct impression one of them had been flirting with him on a visit to Merrylong before her marriage. It stuck in her mind: you could expect more loyalty from a dog ... and get it. Perhaps it was better to stick with that. She hugged the new baby to her and looked out over the scrub. Slowly she was becoming more used to the life, and in an attempt to soften its harshness had given the cows and chickens names and become easier with their handling. She tried to ride, but her eyesight was too poor: the open plain she turned the cows onto was a shimmering foggy wasteland to her. Approaching carts slowly composed themselves out of the heat and haze, heralded by the barking dogs, but they had to be practically on top of her before the image would sharpen and resolve itself.

They had named the property 'The Magormadine' after a local creek, but the impressive name changed nothing, it seemed less and less a possible Merrylong. Alex wove his way skilfully in and out of the monotonous Pilliga scrub with an ease he was becoming renowned for, disappearing into one part and reappearing later at an exact spot and time, easy and smiling, his whip coiled and slung over one shoulder.[6] It was an impenetrable maze to her and it stretched from the house to the horizon like an endless sea.

Life continued monotonous and depressing on their property. The land they had was quite good, but Alex was not careful enough. The solid drudgery it would take to make something out of it was not in him. Every few days he went off into town, 'to buy the paper', but he arrived home desperately drunk, trundling along prone in the back of a neighbour's cart. In a fit of remorse he would then spend his time 'fixing things' around the house, mending latches and broken chairs.[7] To the careful and ambitious Barbara, these uneven bursts of activity were ridiculous. The wonderful charm of Merrylong days seemed to materialize only as an attempt to buy a few days peace. Her silent disapproval permeated the whole house until one day he started talking of droving. It would mean weeks, maybe months away, but it would earn them some money and it was work he enjoyed. He would be able to escape the persistent look of disappointment on her face and convince himself at the same time that he was doing something financially responsible. She was not sure how to react. She would be left in peace with her small boy and her dog, and the crows staring, insolent and threatening, through the back window.

In early 1882 her father-in-law, Alexander Frater, had a major win at the local racetrack with his horse Recovery.[8] Encouraged by this, and sure he was breeding champion racing stock, for the first time he seriously contemplated moving the family to Sydney. They would be basing their fortune on the quality of their horses and moving away from the secure agricultural life they had built up in the colony.

Merrylong symbolized everything stable and prosperous to Barbara, and when it was sold in 1883, a part of her dream for the future vanished. No matter what happened in her own life it had seemed that Merrylong would always be there, solid and reassuring.[9] Now she was pregnant for the second time and not looking forward to the ordeal of giving birth in the bush alone again. Jane Lennard had told her of unbelievable horrors: of pregnant women, exhausted from overwork, dying alone in labour and being found with 'wild pigs eatin' her as I come along', but Barbara had no money for a proper nurse or a doctor from town. At sixty-three the long dusty journey would be too much for her mother – it was Jane or nothing. In September she gave birth to her second son, Robert, with the dreadful Mrs Lennard assisting. She had been shocked to hear her child referred to as the 'new bit of flesh', as if he were expendable and there would be plenty more. It made her feel like an animal and she became less responsive to Alex.[10]

Next year Alex's father won a major race in Sydney with his horse Highland Mary, and the prize money was considerable: 250 sovereigns for the win and a further two thousand pounds because Penelope had backed the horse. They moved from their house in Summer Hill to another suburb, to be closer to the major racecourses. There was a feeling of ebullience and prosperity, and, full of hope and swagger, they commissioned a portrait of the prizewinning mare to hang over the mantlepiece in Surry Hills. For Barbara, if her own life was not working out too well, there was still some security in her parents-in-law.[11]

By Christmas 1884 she was expecting her third child. She could not rely on Alex to take care of the other children at all and hated the thought of asking Mrs Lennard to come again, so she appealed to her elder sister Elizabeth for help. Elizabeth Glover was now a midwife with two children of her own. Her daughter Sarah was a gentle, pretty girl of nineteen, with long auburn hair and a shy and intelligent manner. The sisters decided on an exchange: if Sarah came to help with the children, Barbara would teach her to read and write.[12]

When the girl arrived they discovered they were poles apart. Sarah was reserved, with a quiet motherly manner that was obvious immediately in her handling of the two small boys. A photograph of Barbara taken just before she married suggests a feeling of restlessness and vitality, with her long top lip pulled down, as if to stop herself from making some sardonic remark, and her hands held capable and at the ready in her lap. Despite these differences, in time Barbara and Sarah found their common ground and during a thunderstorm hid under the big kitchen table together, holding the children and giggling with nerves as the huge storm moved toward them.[13]

In June 1885 Barbara's third child was born. She was named Elizabeth Penelope in deference to the grandmothers. The baby was tiny and fragile, and she was the first daughter. Barbara felt an overwhelming sense of protectiveness.

Seven

The countryside around Coonamble was changing slowly and imperceptibly, responding to the onslaught of a long drought. Alex was away most of the time and the elder boy, with no regular father figure, became more precociously manly and protective of his mother. By 1886 young Alec was five, his younger brother Robert, three, and the baby Penelope, as she was always known, a sickly weak child made more dangerously so by the terrible season. Years later Barbara wrote a story that gives an idea of her life then. The story, headed 'Drought Driven', embodies her deepest fear – to be left alone with the children to face a hostile and violent stranger:

The younger boy, in a whisper, asks· where they are going, but the elder, though it is against his manliness, obediently mute, holds her skirt until they pass through the first gate. In the better seasons, seated before his father, he had ridden on the daily round. Despite his childhood, he is a better bush scholar than the mother, who has the reputation of having lost herself in the home paddock.

Both her eyes have scars from many visitations of sandy blight, but straining them she looks back at where she thinks the house is. She stops and in a whisper asks her elder son if he can see any sign of the madman following. He raises his head and tip-toes bravely, but the swift darkness of a moonless nightfall shrouds the plains, and blinds for a time the stars. He shakes his head, then looks for the other gate. Thinks it 'mus' be a little ways further more.' With him for pilot they go on. The baby keeps strangely awake, but the younger boy sleeps. The mother struggles along till she realizes that if she were going straight for the dam either the gate or the fence should be struck by now. 'Mind, mother,' from her pilot prevents a fall over a log. Now that speech is permitted, he inquires is she going to Woods'. When he understands she is making for the dam he tells her she is wrong, and counsels waiting till the moon gets up, then he'll take her straight.

She rests on the log and ponders. Certainly she must be clean off the track, and to continue is wearying foolishness. She does not realise how far she has diverged, and hopes by waiting here she may hear her husband or Larry or the Dummy going home. It is a dead log. Her promised pilot considers it unlikely that snakes may find a home near, owing to the distance from water; but she knows the roots of dead trees are a haunt of death adders, and she goes a few paces further. The pilot sits and holds his brother's head while she unstraps the water and bread from her waist. Facing where she judges the road may be, she seats herself on the ground and pillows the sleeping boy across her limbs. Cradling her wide-awake baby in her arms, pressing her cheek to its hot lips, she tries to soothe it to sleep.

Her guide, counsellor, and comforter looks at the three and feels a sense of responsible guardianship. Returning to the subject of snakes for an illustration that he will not shirk his duty, he draws in his mouth and says, 'My word. My word,' emphatically, 'if any snakes er death-adders cares to come anigh 'ere, I'll soon give 'em billy-oh.' He grinds into the dust the heel of his boot – his intended weapon – which from heel to toe does not measure a span. In the darkness she fancies she can see his little freckled face, prematurely grizzled and hairy, as his speech is precocious. Her eyes glow, and a weak mother's pride warms her sick heart. He mounts the log many times, and strains for sight or sound of father's coming. She tries to make her mate lie down beside his sleeping brother and do likewise, but he as often valiantly declares that he is not sleepy, and that he is going to keep awake till father comes. He cuddles close to her, and if in the weary hours that intervene his head bumps her, the keenness of this resolve immediately rouses him and he jumps up, and mounting the log looks for sign of dilatory moon. When nature conquers his spirit and his head falls, she holds it to her side, thankful that all three sleep.

When the moon blandly, placidly rises, she knows for sure it is long, long past the hour that should bring her husband. Its rising demonstrates also that she is altogether off the home track, and has somehow wandered to the boundary fence between the cultivation paddock and the unfenced, ringbarked country. The moon acting as a mammoth footlight throws into high relief the bleached, bare tree bodies, grotesque and fantastical, like a gathering of fanatical Buddhist giants with paralysed arms raised to heaven, or pointing to the devastation all around.

Another day dawns.

Only butterfly sleep has visited the baby, who in waking with convulsive start disturbs the pilot. His quick wits instantly remember all.

'Woods' land mother,' pointing to the ring-barked trees, and the other two awaken, but she is so cramped that with the baby in her arms it is impossible to move. The pilot tries to help her, then holds baby. She takes a rapid sweeping survey, but it is not quite daylight.

If she has any milk in her sagging breasts for her unweaned baby it would but injure the child. She gives the younger boy a drink from the canteen and a piece of damper, then, taking the baby, bids the pilot help himself. She moistens a piece of bread, and placing it in her mouth tries to feed the baby in bird fashion. Its novelty commends it to the second boy, who asks for a like favor. His brother bird-mothers him.

When again bidden to eat the pilot says, 'I'll wait for you, mother.' From the highest point of the log he vouchsafes his opinion as to the locality of home. While she muses, his quick ears catch the first coo-e-e. 'There's father, mother.' He rushes to the log, throws back his head, wings his mouth with both hands, and coo-e-e's back with all his strength. Louder than hers, for she rises and coo-e-es also.

They are all standing on the log, as though beneath was flooded, for she, now that rescue is assured, is almost paralysed. The husband, though he sees them afar, never ceases to run as if every second that parts them may be fatal. He helps her down and puts his arms round baby and mother, and rests his head for a moment on her shoulder. His wildly-beating heart seems to deafen her. When he can speak he says, 'I hoped you might have gone to Woods'' (their nearest neighbour – eight miles away), 'and went there first. Let's be going.'

'Is the cranky man gone, father?' asks the pilot. The father nods.

But the pilot is voluble, and tells him all about the madman and the snake, and old Baldy's breaking the window. 'Oh!' the father gasps – relief and thankfulness in his voice. 'Then it was the cow

---

broke it.' He would have carried the baby, but she has seen so little of him since her birth that she treats him as a stranger, and hides her head on her mother's breast.

With the younger boy astride his father's neck they go home. Nothing inside has been disturbed. The husband lights a fire. He had brought a quarter of mutton home, but it should have been 'salted down' at once. In such weather meat will not even set. It is thrown out, and they have a tea and damper breakfast.

Larry had managed to bleed a few turgid drops from the Pea-eater, and the brute had staggered to his feet and had been turned into the cultivation paddock, bald and furrowed, but by no plough.

All must camp at the dam. When Larry, who too has been scouring the plain, sees the smoke, he understands and returns to the house. Zero, chased by the madman, has gone down for the last time, and lies in the centre of a circle, which, game to the last, he has kicked in his efforts to rise. His uppermost eye-ball is in the maw, of a crow. His struggles have filled the socket with dust and blood. She washes it, ties a piece of mosquito net over his head, and says 'Good-bye' to him. Baldy stands stock still with unseeing eyes, and has ceased to low. 'I can't leave them like this. In mercy shoot them,' she implores. The rifles are out in the scrub, but Larry sharpens the butcher's knife for Zero. A push sends Baldy down, and an axe ends her sufferings.

They improvise a bush carry-all by securing the tent across two wooden crow-bars. Absolute necessaries are placed on this. There is little of personal linen to take. The whole household resources have for weeks past waited rain in the wash-house. The younger boy climbs, delighted, on the novel conveyance, but the pilot disdains to be carried like a little boy, and gets his stick horse in readiness. There is an old rooster, now blind, that had been the docile playmate of the pilot in his quadruped days. The boy pleads for its inclusion. Instead its neck is wrung. The few other fowls are left to their fate. Very subdued the boy mounts his horse, and suiting its pace to his mother's, trots beside her; shows her where they went off the track last night, and explains how he could have prevented it if he had known she was not going to Woods'. The journey is terrible. The heat waves flicker around, dazzling and searing them. And ever the mocking quicksilver mirage precedes them. Half-way the halting haunches of the pilot's steed show signs of knocking up. Still he

---

scorns a lift. 'You can't carry a man on horseback.' A whip is all he wants. His father gives him a strap, and with it he flogs the last stages out of his thoroughbred colt.

Before them a solitary mount, like a bald head, rises from the plain. The belt of scrub resembles a feathery beard round its throat, with a burst jugular – the now dried gully – expanding into an abscess at the dam.

This is the water they have come for. Stagnant water knows three stages. When it turns milky the taste is peculiarly sweetish, and it is offensive only when 'going down' the throat. If it contains fish their heads will often be seen near the surface. In the second stage it is opalescent. Then it smells and tastes after it is down, and the fish may be seen lengthways near the surface. But in the green, slimy stage, when the dead fish float, it seldom stays down. At every stage it teems with animalculae.

The travellers keep wide of the dam, but even at that distance it smells. The flies and mosquitoes from the water swarm in this timber, rooted in the sand that contains many creeping horrors. The Dummy has a selection here, and has camped all night in the scrub. He has some boiled mutton and a billy of tea ready when they come. The weary mother is anxious, for her baby will swallow only a few mouthfuls of tea, and lies in her lap with half-open eyes and slack lips. While the men pitch the tent she bathes its listless body, and it revives slightly. Meanwhile, the pilot makes a rapid recovery, and becomes wonderfully optimistic anent the natural advantages of this new home. Certainly there are a few more flies, swishing them away from her, and the mosquitoes are 'a bit tonicy,' but they always make you 'sit up' before rain, and he draws his mother's attention to a little cloud overhead, which he feels sure means rain. Anyhow, there's lots of water, no need to carry wood, and there's plenty of meat. Though it's rather early in the season he wouldn't wonder but they'll come across an emu's nest and get the eggs. He stops at this mighty probability as though such a find would more than compensate for any hardships past, present, and to to come.

From the pilot's raincloud a few tepid drops fall like the sweat beads when the dish cover is raised from a hot joint. Then, duty done, the sky clears. At night, inside the door of the tent they burn billy-lids of dried leaves, trying to smoke the mosquitoes out and away. Light as are the baby's slumbers during the night the mother's are lighter.

34

As a result of a conference between the husband, Larry, and the Dummy, the dam – its depths having been gauged – is to be wired round with wire drawn from the fences. It is a hard day's work for all three. This barrier signifies that the struggle to feed and water the sheep is at an end. Many of them thrust their heads through the wires and fall so. Their upturned heads pilloried between the wires suggest consideration for the crows.

The men are thoughtful for the mother. She hardly takes her eyes from the pinched face of her baby, whom the pilot's best efforts fail to attract. The infant's burning, restless head moves from side to side. She dozes with wide-open eyes, and moans continuously. The nearest town is 40 or 50 miles away. No possibility of bringing help thence.

A road leading to a squatter's homestead divides the plain below the dam. Along this towards evening a pair drive seated in a buggy. The husband cooees and runs towards it. They pull up and wait for him. It is the squatter and his young wife from Sydney, where they have been for months waiting for the drought to break. They are returning merely to investigate. The gaunt, hollow-eyed man beside the buggy in some respects resembles the perishing animals around. He tells the lady of his sick child and asks will she come to see it. He leads the way. The baby has had a convulsive fit, and the mother has it in a bucket of warm water. She wraps a blanket round its wee body, half of which seems transparent. The city lady does not know what to do, but remarks, 'Oh, the blanket is too rough for its skin. Let me help you put on its nightgown,' taking up its soiled garment gingerly. The mother, holding the baby to her scarcely beating heart, shakes her head. 'Can I do anything for you? Would you like some eau-de-cologne?' asks the lady. The mother looks into the eyes of this childless woman, and she, with an uncomfortable feeling, goes back to the buggy. She remarks, 'Oh, Roger, I'm sure that poor little baby will die, and I feel certain its mother has not even a clean nightgown to lay it out if it does. She has such a strange look about her, and when I offered her some scent she looked so queer that I came away. Drive quickly,' she says, with her perfumed handkerchief to her nose, as they pass the dam.

She is merely thoughtless from inexperience. There are so many who would fain gallop away from any hint of starvation.

In her recollection of the times, Barbara had left one important person out. Sarah Glover stayed with the family for a year.[1] In late 1886 Barbara rose early one morning to take some eggs to market and returned to find Alex and Sarah together. He had been away droving and Barbara had not seen much of him since the birth of her daughter; when she had seen him, relations were strained. Life was getting much more difficult and she resented him. Sensing her disapproval, he gravitated toward Sarah who, gentle and susceptible, could not say no.

They lived for a while in an uneasy truce and then Alex suggested Barbara go to Sydney with the children for her 'health' and a change of air. She accepted the offer. He gave her a cheque to cover her expenses and in March 1887 she left.[2] It is possible she was worried to the point of real illness; she had always been anxious about her age – youth was a prize in women as in brood mares, and Sarah was nine years younger. Once in Sydney she stayed with her parents-in-law in Surry Hills.

While living in Sydney, Alex's father had invested money in another property in northern New South Wales. He sought advice from a solicitor and gave him ten thousand pounds to buy and run the property, in case the family wanted to move back on the land.[3] While he enjoyed the success of his racehorses, and his family liked the city life, he still wrote 'grazier' when asked his occupation. Nevertheless he had moved at the right time: the drought in the country was so severe they were lucky to have an alternative.

Fanny, the illegitimate daughter of their eldest son, ohn, had moved to Sydney with the Fraters and was making fu l use of her unusual position in the family. She was a naughty observant little girl, allowed to be different because of her ancestry, and sympathized with and forgiven for the same reason. Her memories remain like sudden spotlights on the domestic doings of the family. No sooner had Penelope bought a pair of candlesticks from an auction of Henry Parkes's possessions, than the prisms that hung round the edge to reflect the light were hooked off and taken outside to start fires. When Barbara arrived, she found after a few days that some of the money she had brought with her was gone. She blamed Fanny for it, took her outside and put her up in a tree – where Fanny hung, riddled with guilt, loudly proclaiming her innocence.[4]

When Barbara went to present Alex's cheque, it was returned to her dishonoured. She packed her things and went back home to Coonamble, but the place was deserted: Alex had fled to Narrabri with Sarah.[5]

Barbara had one close friend from her governess days, Elizabeth, the elder Frater daughter. She had been a witness at Barbara's wedding and had met her own husband on her way to visit Alex and Barbara. She was now living on a large property in the north of New South Wales and somehow heard of her brother's flight to Narrabri. She went down to reason with him. He had registered under a false name at a local hotel, but Sarah had been nervous and asked the landlady not to say she was there if anyone asked for her. It made the woman suspicious: Sarah was visibly pregnant.

When Barbara arrived in town Alex immediately bundled Sarah into a carriage going north to Walgett, staying to face the music for a few days before he followed her. Barbara was left in Narrabri alone. She went several times to question the innkeeper with Elizabeth, but the woman was adamant: they had registered as man and wife, and the girl was enceinte; had she known they were not married she would not have allowed them to stay.[6]

It is not clear where Barbara went after this. Sarah Glover eventually gave birth to her child and Alex was faced with an added responsibility. The property at Magormadine Creek was drought-stricken and unproductive, so he sold it, for a poor price, and went back to droving and shearing, leaving Sarah with his brothers in Queensland. If, in the confusion of his rapidly multiplying family, he looked to his father for financial assistance, he was asking at the wrong time.[7]

Alexander's solicitor had lost all the money given him. Taking his horses to a country racetrack one day, Alexander had stopped off to inspect the place where his property should have been and found nothing. He quickly brought the solicitor to court, but the man suicided and no money was ever recovered. He was forced to sell his house in Sydney and buy another property to provide his family with an income. He had little money left over and the property he bought at Deep Creek near Narrabri was inferior, but he packed up and arrived there one morning in a spring cart with all his family and ninepence in his pocket. Right back where he started.

It is not clear where Barbara was living at this point, but it is likely that she stayed with a succession of relatives – always an inconvenience and a financial burden. Her young daughter, Penelope, stayed with Barbara's mother, Elizabeth Lawrence, in Scone. Barbara was very short of money. Forced to earn her living any way she could, she travelled around selling Bibles door to door, using every inch of her personality to make a sale. In a fit of revenge, she told a prospective buyer that her father-in-law had thrown her out with her three children, because she was a Catholic. Her listener was sympathetic: Catholic himself, he bought a Bible and berated Alexander Frater when next he saw him. Alexander was furious, but Barbara had won a double point in both irritating her father-in-law and selling a Bible.

Under pressure from the scandalous split in her family, caused in part by her own daughter, Elizabeth Glover now arranged a meeting between Alex and Barbara at her own house. Barbara drove there in a buggy, arriving hot and dusty but determined to swallow her pride and make peace. Alex was adamant: he loved Sarah and he would stay with her. Exhausted and humiliated Barbara jumped to her feet, blurted out 'You stupid man!' and slapped his face. The marriage was over.[8]

Eight

With little money coming in and three young children Barbara had now to make a proper living or receive support. Five months later, in August 1887, she sued Alex for maintenance. He resented being brought into the court and opposed the petition, using as his reason the fact that he already had a child by 'another woman in town' and had, therefore, enough children to support! The magistrate at once awarded Barbara five shillings a week, noting Alex's outrageous statement in his written account of the proceedings.[1] Alex would have been quite happy to leave things as they were – and he had the weight of his family's opinion behind him. As far as his father, Alexander Frater, was concerned his son was always right, no matter what, and Penelope was now too numbed by the blows fate had dealt her to raise serious objection. But Alex was busily starting a whole new family with Sarah, and it was left to Penelope Frater to show Barbara what kindness she could to placate her. She offered to keep the children while Barbara went off to earn her living. Barbara accepted the offer for her two sons, and one morning she brought the boys to Deep Creek, leaving the eldest to cry himself to sleep that night, with an awful feeling of helplessness and despair he never forgot.[2]

Barbara finally found a small milliner's shop in the far north of the state in a mining town called Emmaville, and there she began to tie exquisite bows onto bonnets and train her mind to accommodate the ridiculous trivia of her new profession. Business was slow. The main interest in the town was tin and silver, not hats.

Alexander Frater had taken out a bookmaker's licence and was touring New South Wales taking bets, to augment the yield from the property at Deep Creek. Penelope, shaken by their reduced circumstances, had become cautious with every penny and was making her own butter and travelling around the district in a cart, selling it in rancid bundles to her neighbours. Their favourite son was in trouble and they didn't want to add to their burdens by the scandal and expense of any more legal proceedings. As long as both parties could be mollified it seemed politic to keep things as they were.[3] This left Barbara in a worse situation than when she had married into the Frater family. Her position in the world was unclear and humiliating – neither wife nor maid – and in addition the maintenance money from Alex was irregular and then stopped altogether. With her millinery business as bad as it was, she relied on the money from Alex and travelled back to Narrabri to claim her arrears. The useless result was that Alex was put in gaol. As usual, his father was outraged and had special food sent in from a restaurant to feed his son. He blamed Barbara entirely, even though imprisonment was clearly against her interests.

Barbara arrived at Deep Creek at dawn one morning to collect her children from a household that had, by now, become quite hostile. Fanny, ten years old and working hard for her keep, was out in the yard baling cows with Alec and Robert when Barbara arrived. She stood in the middle of the road with her hair streaming down, denouncing the Fraters. 'Here am I – the foxes have holes, the birds of the air have nests; but I have nowhere to lay my head.' And, collecting her mud-spattered little boys, one in each hand, she started to walk back to Narrabri, with one parting shot: 'I am going away, homeless, friendless, destitute.'

She took them to a hotel in Narrabri, and soon the whole town heard the story. The Fraters were furious: she hadn't even waited to clean up the children![4] Things could get no worse. Barbara decided to divorce.

It was a brave and unusual choice. The law had only recently been changed and very few people had taken advantage of the new freedom to end a marriage. The feeling was still that the die was cast with the original marriage vow and you lived with the consequences. Religion was still very much part of everyday life. Divorce carried a stigma of shame and amorality, especially for the woman involved. Barbara had been avoiding it as long as she could, as much for the pain it would cause Penelope as for the impossible expense and the humiliation of having the whole story dragged out in court. But the alternative was unappealing: never to be able to remarry and to remain linked to a man now totally alienated from her. The Fraters seemed to believe it was their prerogative to absorb her children into their family, as they had absorbed other 'mistakes' their sons had made. That was the final straw. She went back to Emmaville determined to fight for them and her right to a clear future, unencumbered by an uncaring and improvident husband.

She had exaggerated her position in the heat of the moment when she was standing in the road. She was not homeless, but pretty near friendless, and fighting off destitution with her earnings from her tiny millinery in a bleak part of northern New South Wales. She initiated divorce proceedings with the utmost economy – but Alex was hard to find.

On 23 October 1888 Edward Ellis, bailiff's assistant, served a citation on him 'after considerable difficulty', describing him as a grazier of Boggabilla, adding 'late' of Boggabilla before he even sent a copy off to the Supreme Court in Sydney. Barbara was describing him by 13 November as 'of no fixed address or occupation or place of residence and constantly moving about'. She believed he had no intention of defending the suit and a 'great deal of time and expense would be incurred were it necessary to serve the respondent with notice of further proceedings ... owing to the difficulty of ascertaining his whereabouts.'[5]

After the birth of their first child Alex had left Sarah with his brothers in Queensland so he could travel to find work. His father wanted him to fight the divorce, but it was an expensive and unnecessary procedure to him, and he avoided meeting the bailiffs at all costs. These delays were extremely difficult for Barbara. Six months after she had asked for her case to be heard without him there was still no progress, and her solicitor sent a hurrying letter to the Supreme Court stating that she was 'in very poor circumstances' and, unless they could hear the case 'directly', it was likely to be postponed indefinitely for lack of funds.

In 1889 she went to Sydney armed with affidavits from the innkeeper, Mrs Everingham, and the magistrate at Narrabri, having been given permission for their testimonies to be heard 'in absentia', due to the expense of having to transport them to the court in Sydney. It had taken a year for her case to be heard. On 5 August she went into court and asked for custody of the children and all costs to be awarded against Alex. All issues were decided in her favour. She was handed a piece of paper that forbade her to remarry until the decree became absolute. And was free.

It was the four-hundred-and-fifty-first divorce in the colony, which had previously only allowed separations through the church or by special Act of Parliament for each individual case. The Matrimonial Causes Act had changed the primitive legal status of people wanting to separate who, until then, only had permission to leave each other and 'not render conjugal rights'. There was still prurient interest in divorce, but luckily little fuss was made about her case in the papers, and the court reporter wrote only a brief outline for the *Sydney Morning Herald*. There were more exotic happenings in a neighbouring court: a Mrs Mayhinch was accused of poisoning her husband.

On the legal paper she had to sign as final proof of her divorce, she started to write 'Barbara Lawrence', as if the whole marriage was wiped away and she was back to her maiden status in name as well, then she corrected herself and wrote 'Frater' over her mistake. But she was Frater in name only and when, six months later, she signed another legal document, she described herself as 'widow', and so she was.[6] She never referred to Alex again and never allowed the children to speak of him. She buried the pain and humiliation as completely as she could and proceeded with the next phase of her life. But while she hid the rejection from herself and her family, it remained in her character: she didn't trust easily, and bitterly denounced the foolishness of people who allowed themselves to be exploited.

'If you make yourself a doormat, don't be surprised if you're walked on', became a favourite expression of warning to her daughter, and when her sons began to show signs of their father's character she reacted with scorn and ferocity to stamp it out. If the ordeal set her character with more grimness than was expected in a woman, it gave her confidence in her powers to endure, and made her a practical and thoughtful friend in later life, when her own security was assured. But the dark Celtic streak in her was more profound after the divorce from Alex and surfaced later in ugly rages and bursts of suspicion and melancholy for which she was always desperately apologetic afterwards. She loved to sing bleak Scottish dirges, to the horror of her grandchildren, and was more at home now with fear and loneliness than pleasure and affection.[7] It was a cruel trick played on the bright scornful girl she had been, but if she could have seen into Alex and Sarah's future she might have been glad she had picked herself up and briskly headed off in the opposite direction.

To pay for her trip to Sydney and to house her while she was there, Barbara had taken a job as housekeeper for a doctor in Woollahra. It was light work and he was a well-respected man with a house full of antique furniture and porcelain. It is not clear where she had left the children, though as a rule Penelope stayed with her grandmother Elizabeth Lawrence in Scone. She didn't tell him about the divorce, going about her work with growing enjoyment. The house was full of light and delicacy. Dr Baynton treated her well; she was in the city; she had what she had come for; and at thirty-three she was still young.

Nine

From the time of her return to Coonamble and the discovery
of her husband's desertion, Barbara's life took a divergent
path from Sarah Glover's. For Barbara it was the crisis that
propelled her out of one life and into another that nourished
her mind and body for the rest of her days. For Sarah it was
the beginning of the end.

Often the photographs and drawings of another century
awake a feeling of wistfulness, a longing to belong to another
age, when perhaps things were more elegant and benign. If a
portrait survived of Sarah, it would probably show her as her
daughter remembered her: a pretty woman with red-blonde
hair and a shy and evasive look, a slight figure, slender and
frail, dressed in the clothes of the time which emphasized her
small waist and slender arms.[1] Looking at her life one cannot
be anything but pleased to be squarely in another century.

For Sarah, the friendship with Barbara had been important.
The Lawrences were proud but poor, with few prospects of
improvement other than marriage. As Sarah's mother could
neither read nor write, Barbara was offering Sarah a chance to
inch herself up the social scale as she herself had done. Even
if she was only partly educated, she could become a governess,
which would open up a world otherwise unavailable to her.
The age was not kind to young girls with little money trying
to find security and the propriety of marriage, and the bond
between the two women was strengthened by Barbara's wit,
which made light of the dangers of the outside world.[2]

Sarah was sensitive, gentle and orthodox, a joy to have
around the house and good with the children. Her presence
meant freedom for Barbara, who lost no time in making use
of it, going off to picnic races and often staying away for a day

or so, leaving her young niece in charge of the children. Alex Frater was not a man to be trusted, niece or no niece. The men in his family had an instinctive attitude to sex, to put it mildly. His parents' marriage had been based on a magnetic sexual attraction. His mother, at sixteen, had been so besotted with her young man she was willing to renounce all security for him and march up the aisle while her father publicly washed his hands of her as the service was being performed. In married life, she had only kept her husband in check by rubbing in her better breeding whenever he got out of hand, which was often. Their sons, insulated by the prosperity and support of their parents, did precisely as they liked. With classic double standards, Alexander Frater senior locked up his own daughters securely but poor Sarah Glover, from the unimportant Lawrence family, was an easy mark.

When her husband suggested Barbara take a trip to Sydney, he was hoping to slip away quietly with Sarah, who, travelling with him to Narrabri, must have felt a deep sense of shame. This was exacerbated when they were discovered together at the hotel. Alex, on the other hand, was treating the whole thing with larrikin scorn, using the name of the local policeman as a pseudonym. It did not bode well for the relationship. When her baby was born, Sarah resented it, and despite her motherly nature never became close to the little girl. She must have been relieved, after the attempted reconciliation, that Alex stayed with her, but she never forgave the brutality with which he had changed her life.[3]

In the beginning Sarah was sent to stay with the Frater brothers in Queensland, while Alex moved about shearing and droving. She had no house of her own, little money, and was not yet officially married. When they finally had a place of their own in a remote part of northern New South Wales, Alex still preferred working away, leaving Sarah with her ever-growing family. In 1891 she had her twenty-fifth birthday and her second child, a boy called Walter. By the turn of the century she had six children, delivered mostly by her mother while Alex was away – and her hair had turned completely white.

Her children grew up a loyal and devoted little band,

intensely protective of their mother, fearful of the scenes that followed whenever Alex returned home. Sarah had developed a strong religious faith to cope with her adversities and would sit the family at her feet every night to listen to their prayers, covering their hands with hers and returning to her chair afterward to stare down at her brood.[4]

Despite his frequent absences, the children loved their father. Ready to please them in every way, he was sentimental and attentive. The little girl that had been born at the turn of the century, Penelope, was his favourite, and he held her so tight the child had to be taken away from him for fear he'd crush her. They admired his long treks up and down the country, bringing livestock from Brisbane over a thousand miles to market in Sydney, and listened to his stories with excitement. But 'Papa was a waster', and life was hard when he was away.

For weeks, even months, Sarah was left alone. She had been reduced to such despair she had written a letter to Penelope Frater describing her situation and asking for help. Penelope sent her a brisk letter with a five pound note and a bolt of cotton, calling her a hussy and telling her never to write again. Sarah swallowed her pride enough to accept the gift but showed her spirit in refusing to cater to Mrs Frater's elegances when she called one day. She stayed indoors, forcing Penelope to drive all the way up to the house, get out and knock on the door. Most women, aware of Mrs Frater's ancestry, hurried down to the gate to meet her.[5] It may have been this display of hauteur that sparked her interest in Sarah and culminated in a friendship between the two women.

By the beginning of the century news of Barbara's successes were filtering inland from Sydney, and some of her stories had appeared in the *Bulletin* and the *Sydney Morning Herald*. Sarah was distressed and disoriented by the thought of it. There was Barbara, out of the heat and poverty in Sydney, while she, who had supposedly won the prize, laboured under an impossible burden of poverty and childrearing. She blamed herself bitterly for her position. The sound of Barbara's laughter was what she remembered most about her, and she heard it too often. Alex would find on his return a sullen and unresponsive wife who didn't want and couldn't cope with any more children, who felt the act itself and therefore, by association, her husband, had been the cause of all her pain and suffering. Cut off and confused by this reaction, he began to drink more heavily – even more when he realized he was also losing the respect of his children. His charm still pleased the girls in his family, and long after he had abandoned them they remembered it and forgave him, but his sons did not. By then he had a reputation as the town drunk. The boys often had to pick him up and bring him home in the buggy after a binge, and he still gambled too much. One day, in a hopeless gesture of affection, he had brought home a large set of bedroom furniture for Sarah after a big win at the races. She burst into tears: what good was a dressing table when you had no food?

She began to grow noticeably neurotic, clinging to the hope that her children would vindicate her actions. But everything was measured by Barbara. Sarah's sixth child, Penelope, remembers her mother standing for a moment by the window saying, 'She had a Penelope ... and I have a Penelope.' When this girl began to write essays and short stories, Sarah was thrilled and kept them all carefully in a drawer. Confiding in this child later, she said of the beginning of her affair with Alex, 'I tried to stop him – I said no, no ... but he wouldn't listen.'

By 1908 she had two more children, bringing the family to eight – four boys and four girls – and it was a terrible burden for both of them. Alex was away droving now for two years at a stretch, and he sent no money back. Conditions were so bad that their grandmother Penelope Frater kept the family at these times, and it was difficult for all concerned. The children who, despite everything, had never been starved for affection, were a boisterous and lively lot, but their grandmother was strict and pious and she tried to impose her standards on them. One afternoon she readied herself for her nap, giving two little Frater girls set pieces of her Bible to read while she slept. They waited patiently till she fell asleep and then shot off outside. She woke in a fury to find her Bible abandoned and shouts coming from the fowlyard.[6]

The family had moved to Baan Baa, another property south

of Narrabri given to Alex by his father. The children went to the local school and the whole neighbourhood was well aware of the financial trouble they were in. Sarah had to suffer the scornful looks and sarcasm of the local shopkeeper, who sent the children home with loud contemptuous reminders to 'tell your mother to pay this bill'. The whole district put what they needed 'on tick', and it gave the storeman power to be pleasant or unpleasant as he chose.

At school a couple of the children's friends looked suspiciously like them. Alex had settled several old scores with his neighbours by seducing their wives.[7] The children grew up to accept these children as their half-brothers and sisters, but none of this did much for Sarah's self-esteem, and when one day she sent her daughter Penelope to bring Alex home after one of his rampages, the little girl took the opportunity to tick him off. He was sitting next to her, still drunk, a huge shambling form bumping along in the cart. With childish lucidity she enumerated his faults and described in detail the effect it was having on her mother. To her horror he burst into tears, mumbling 'She was the only one I ever loved . . . the only one.' And he was losing her.

In 1908 she became pregnant again, for the ninth time. Alex was away and Sarah had gone to stay with her mother, giving birth to the little boy under a cherry tree not far from the house. It stretched her limited resources to the breaking point. Her children couldn't remember a time now when her hair had been anything other than white, and they stared in amazement at the lock of auburn hair their father kept entwined in a watch chain.[8]

She was taken away one day, exhausted and disturbed, to a psychiatric hospital in Sydney. Her youngest boy cried, but whether it was because his mother was being driven away or because the wheels of her buggy were perilously close to his kittens he couldn't afterwards remember.

For a while she improved and was sent home, but the sight of the property sent her straight back into despair and she was returned to the hospital. Alex brought her last-born down to Sydney to see her, but Sarah's condition did not improve, and while the child never forgot the sight of his mother in a red flannel nightgown, she continued to deteriorate. The news of her death came suddenly, and she was brought up to Narrabri to be buried in the cemetery there.

For Alex this was the last in a long sequence of terrible events. He had been a loved, easy-going member of a large, well-to-do family, totally unprepared for what was to come. The drive for improvement had not been bred in him as it had in his parents, and even their will and tenacity had not prevented fate from taking away most of what they had so laboriously put together. Spoiled and talented, Alex had never had to push himself to achieve anything and when the time came he couldn't see the need. If his parents had difficulty maintaining a reasonable way of life he, with no internal drive and no more financial help from them, soon collapsed into drunkenness and despair.

For a while he continued working, leaving the children at home to be fed by de Kloot, a rabbit-trapper who came round and baked damper for them. Their grandmother Penelope Frater was by then over seventy, and she did not offer to have them at Deep Creek. At night they huddled away from the window, sending a deputy up to see if there was 'anyone out there moving about'.[9] Finally Alex fell apart completely, sold the property, abandoned the children, and went bush.

They lost touch with him. Still a magnificent rider, he found work around the countryside, and later one of his daughters discovered him working as a 'useful' on a property near Sydney. The children he had left behind suffered terribly as a result of his abandoning them, travelling from one sullen relative to another, hoping to be taken in. They were regarded as an imposition by families already hard-pressed, often arriving by train at one destination to be unceremoniously bundled back on board and returned to where they had come from. In later life none of the children allowed their harsh memories to destroy them, creating professional lives and careers for themselves out of force of necessity. Years later the youngest daughter, Belle, stepping brightly in front of a line of oncoming traffic, believed they would all stop for her 'because she was a Frater'.

Sarah's legacy to her children was the affection and

gentleness she had given them. Barbara's life would lead to great financial security, but relations with her family suffered. Reacting violently to the harshness of her bush experience, she pursued security with a single-mindedness that inevitably led to sacrifice, but she survived. Alex often spoke of his three eldest children with regret and tenderness. Barbara, twice spurned by him, would not have allowed him anywhere near them. He remained in their minds as a shameful, shadowy creature, put aside.

Ten

The lack of publicity at the time of her divorce allowed Barbara to live her life as naturally as she wanted, without scandal or notoriety. She was working as a housekeeper for a sixty-nine-year-old doctor in Woollahra, a pretty, tree-lined part of Sydney. She had not told him she had three children and was already creating a past for herself that suited her better. She painted in the background to this new picture by claiming that her father was a 'clerk in holy orders'.[1] The 'clerk' was by then a charcoal-burner on the plains outside Narrabri.

Dr Baynton was a well-read, educated man, thoughtful and orderly, and she desperately wanted him to think well of her. There could be no greater contrast with her ex-husband, Alex, than this elderly surgeon. For one thing, the feeling of indiscriminate sexuality that had been part of her life with Alex was certainly no part of Thomas Baynton's. Although no portraits of Dr Baynton seem to have survived, we have a few indications of his life and personality. His father had been sent out to Australia by his family because he had married Eliza Smith, the local innkeeper's daughter. In accordance with family tradition, he had taken a degree in medicine before his arrival in the colony in 1840. Over the next thirty years he worked on the land until his death in 1872, when he left his four children substantial parcels of property with the proviso that his eldest son, Thomas, also take a degree in medicine before he inherited his share of the Baynton holdings, Darlington Station in Victoria.

Over difficult and turbulent years in the colony Thomas had guided his family's fortunes through drought and depression to bring him to his present position as a wealthy doctor. After the death of his first wife he had remained single, but maintained a wide circle of friends, which included links with the old country and a network of contacts in London and Scotland. He increased his knowledge of antiques until, in 1890, his collection included fine china, porcelain and eastern prayer rugs. Like many men of his time he was interested in woodwork and had made a number of pieces of simple furniture around the house.

Despite her position in the house as a domestic servant, Barbara maintained the air of aloofness and dignity that she had first cultivated at Merrylong. She believed that the running of the household, with all its monotony, was part of a greater good that should be generally acknowledged, especially if she was doing it. In an article on domestic service she wrote later, Barbara stated her belief that cleanliness was next to Godliness, and that good food 'had much to do with the making of a Christian' – even a bored Christian.[2] Her image of her own femininity had taken a severe blow, and, though still slender and attractive, she continued to understate her age. It must have been a strange household, with the wiry, enigmatic young woman going about her business briskly, and the old doctor gradually realizing he could not put this employee into the category of 'servant' as easily as he would have thought.

For her part she was beginning to realize what opportunities were becoming available to her. Gone was the harsh desperate environment she had survived in for the last few years. The house in Woollahra was the antithesis of the glare and dust, wood and tin that had surrounded her: it protected her and filtered out the memories when they came.

She became a companion, listening to him whenever he spoke about the antiques he collected, the woodwork he did, his practice – and by 1890 he had proposed to her. She set the date for their marriage for 5 March 1890, the day after her divorce was made final. In the marriage register she defiantly wrote 'widow' and 'gentlewoman' in the column marked 'rank or profession'.

Barbara had not told him about her children, and now, at seventy, Dr Baynton had to contend with a noisy young family used to the freedom of the bush.

She introduced him to Penelope first. Five years old, dark

and sloe-eyed, she enchanted him at once. Then came the boys. They found the disciplined city life a great change from their recent past, and the cramped quarters under the sharply sloping roof of the Woollahra house claustrophobic and exasperating. The bedrooms were on the top floor, one on either side of the roof tree. The only light came through large dormer windows at the end.

Dr Baynton wanted his way of life preserved so he introduced harsh disciplinary measures to curb their flamboyance. Barbara always sided with her new husband: she had come to her safe harbour and the children had to recognize that and be grateful. She would not jeopardize her position for them or anyone and, as a result, relations with her sons slowly changed. Robert, the younger boy, who most resembled his father, began to draw away from her. If it was the price she had to pay for her new life, she paid it and moved on.

The three children were very different. Barbara had kept the youngest, Penelope, with her as much as possible and the little girl now became the darling of the household, spoilt by Dr Baynton and indulged by her brothers. Although Barbara loved children in the abstract, she had had to fight too hard for hers and now wanted something for herself, with as little trouble as possible. They were never given toys of any description, their mother remarking that 'all a child needed was a cardboard box and a little imagination'.[3] It was all she had had. But Alec, the elder boy, thought Penelope needed a doll and carved one out of a piece of wood for her. He loved his mother quietly and devotedly and extended this affection to his sister, Penelope, with a sweetness and placidity that only earned him the derisive nickname 'Lappy' in return. His younger brother, Robert, was much more boisterous and energetic, but even his high spirits could not protect him from his mother's scathing tongue. She nicknamed him 'Weed', because he 'was such a tall thin boy and grew so fast'. 'Lappy' and 'Weed' carried their nicknames into full adult life and died within eighteen months of each other, having been through two world wars still carrying these preposterous names. They were never spoken to as children; no nursery books were bought; no fairy tales read – it was Dickens or nothing.[4]

As Barbara settled into her new life, the reality of her past did not fade, but grew more and more stark in contrast to the life she was now leading. There were a few minor problems. Dr Baynton had a wide circle of friends, and the transition from housekeeper to wife was not a simple one, but she was eager to please and used to greater hazards. Dr Baynton taught her more about the antiques he had collected, and the enjoyment he got from their style and elegance was catching. As her knowledge grew she began to see the difference between the heavy elaborate designs that engulfed Victorian life and the light sparse economy of the Regency period. The two can be seen side by side in glaring juxtaposition in a graveyard in Ashfield near the second house she was to live in in Sydney: the heavy Victorian swathes and swirls next to the elegant simplicity of smooth, rounded sandstone. She quickly came to feel she was living in an over-crowded age of 'Victorian rubbish' and, under Dr Baynton's supervision, never collected anything from this period that she intended to keep, or put on show.[5] She began to surround herself with materials and designs that depicted a gentler natural world. Fantastic birds in dazzling plumage sat on twisted vines embroidered on her curtains, and spring flowers in sharp, bright colours were printed on the material on her chairs. In glass cabinets, cherubic china faces stared out, and moulded fruits sat on the smooth wood surfaces her husband had carved. Nevertheless, however much she surrounded herself with this revised world, the bush would not go away.

Now that she had lost her family of in-laws and was totally alienated from Penelope Frater, Barbara drew her own family about her. Her sister Mary Ann, who had been a witness to this marriage, came to stay, and her mother came down from Scone. The mother–daughter relationship was a primary one in Barbara's life. She needed Elizabeth to bring back memories of the care and protection she had had as a child and help her with her own children, who were in strange array around her, reeling from the fierce demands she made on their loyalty.

The maternal bond had become more important to Barbara during the disintegration of her first marriage, when it had been one of the few constants. While it is not clear if she saw much of Elizabeth Lawrence during this time, the bond between the two remained firm throughout, despite what Barbara saw as the treacherous behaviour of her sisters. When Dr Baynton gave her an edition of Bacon's essays, she underlined various sentences and added comments in pencil. In the essay 'Of Revenge', the sentence ' "You shall read," saith he, "that we are commanded to forgive our enemies, but you never read that we are commanded to forgive our friends" ' a thin wavering line to the bottom of the page has added 'or relations'. But this wariness did not include her mother. Maternal love was fundamental love and a love that she was now finding it hard to pass on unconditionally to her own children.

Nevertheless her mother's visits were not a success. At seventy, Elizabeth felt herself too old to play an active role in anything and, haunted by memories of her own past, she trotted mournfully off to church alone every day. The children stepped gingerly around her as she sat glumly in a corner with her Bible, swathed in clouds of Protestant gloom.[6] Finally she went back to Scone, to the comforting routine of her own house and the bossy ministrations of her other daughters.

Eleven

Through the 1890s, marriage to Dr Baynton provided Barbara with a background that was stable and stimulating. She had no financial worries and, though not hugely rich, Dr Baynton was careful and steady: there would be no sudden reverses while he was in charge. 'Two can't drive the buggy' was a favourite saying of Barbara's to her daughter, and she was glad to have someone take over the reins.[1] It meant her world was calm and orderly, and in this peace she had the time to assimilate her past. In the quiet of the early morning before the household woke, memories surged back.

While she was attempting to make some sense out of the disorder of her past, Dr Baynton was leading her into a new world. He set a standard of discipline and intellectual activity that was always a little beyond Barbara's immediate grasp, and she loved him for it.

As a character, Dr Baynton must have had something of his forebears' fire, coupled with a natural inclination toward caution and husbandry, and a great love of beauty. A strong and disciplined old man, he loved darkness and the night. Given the veiled sensuality in her poems about him, it seems their feelings were mutual and not exclusively on an intellectual level, and though Dr Baynton was not a young man, Barbara was at the peak of her physical attractiveness. The years had made her thin and pale, and this slight and embattled look gave her a neatness and fragility that suited her features. Though later she would be described as positively ugly, she was close to beauty now.

Perhaps in thanks for his security Dr Baynton had become too subservient to the strict moral code of his church, but it was important to him and Barbara fell into step beside him.

The story of her father being a 'clerk in holy orders' may have had its origins in her desire to please him. No one ever contradicted her on this point, and John Lawrence was far enough out of her life now to have been a wandering tribesman in Outer Mongolia if she'd wanted him to be.

She had already shown an instinctive appreciation of china when, stumbling on some piece of crockery in Coonamble, she had sent Alec outside with some soap to scrub all the dirt and grime away. Feeling the smooth clean surface, she could tell if it were soft or hard paste and make a guess as to the factory it was made in.[2] She had made money on these early windfalls, and now Dr Baynton pushed her knowledge to the point where she began to be properly expert.

A small monogrammed book of Barbara's survives with a list and description of each antique in the Baynton house. Under its heading – plates, bowls, vases, and so on – every piece is identified, and its corresponding mark drawn in. From time to time the name of a previous owner is also noted, such as two dishes with Japanese figures from Rose Scott and three fawn Wedgwood mugs with white ferns from Sir Henry Parkes. An item in the miscellaneous section highlights Barbara's change in circumstance: number 81 was a small peachwood vase with ivory stem and ebony base, 'turned by Dr Baynton' – a far cry from the tappings of the coffin-maker.

Looking down the list of Baccarat glass and Sevres, Chelsea, Dresden and Worcester porcelain, it is obvious that Dr Baynton's collection was extensive and of high quality, and the order Barbara brought into her appreciation of it was part of her growing awareness of precision in her dealings. She began a lifelong habit of scrutiny in matters legal and monetary. Again this was a determined denial of Alex Frater, with his light, vacillating temperament and indifference to all economic facts, save his accounts at the pub and the racetrack. If this careful shepherding of the family's affairs didn't seem quite so obvious a gesture of affection toward her children, it was at least twice as effective. Barbara was drawing the perimeters of her character with neater and firmer lines to fit in with her position.

Dr Baynton introduced her to his circle of friends, which

included interesting and active men and women who were part of the bustling world of Sydney in the 1890s. He gave her careful instructions on correct procedure, and she reacted predictably by absorbing the manners and forms of etiquette too precisely for them to appear to be completely natural. She had crests put on her writing paper and stuck too rigidly to the polite forms of address and reply. She was very aware of the world she had escaped and was not going to be seen to be out of step with her new one.

Sydney had become a popular destination for writers, actors, singers and playwrights, so that the names Barbara had read in the papers and magazines from Europe that formed so much of her early reading, and helped her visualize the great other world, arrived one after another. Dion Boucicault, Robert Louis Stevenson and Rudyard Kipling all visited Sydney, and Sarah Bernhardt played *La Dame aux Camellias* at Her Majesty's – in French. Though she received a 'huge response' to her 'gestures and facial expressions and the great beauty of her voice' it did not escape some critics that these were perhaps not the only qualities necessary in great acting. Sydney itself received mixed reviews, Robert Louis Stevenson stating that he liked it 'if not for itself, for its bits of old London and Paris' and Mark Twain, arriving several years later, said that 'after much oh-ing and ah-ing in admiration' of the spacious, beautiful harbour, he had concluded that Sydney was 'an English city with American trimmings'.

Visiting dignitaries or no, Sydney was growing fast and changing inwardly and outwardly at an extraordinary rate. The city showed its prosperity in a sea of imposing brick warehouses, and in the harbour, as evidence of its past and future, sailships and steamers rode their anchors side by side at Circular Quay.

The fashions of the time featured bustles and whipped-in waists, gloves, and pert hats set on top of short fringes and high upswept hair. The neck, waist and hips were emphasized: the overall effect was tailored and feminine. Barbara suited these clothes quite well, her small bone structure being part of an ideal figure for women, but her hair didn't quite conform to the queenly dignity of contemporary portraits. In most photographs it looks as if she has stood in the wind for a while, having spent a few brisk moments with a brush just before.

Despite women's generally prim appearance, the question of suffrage was receiving widespread publicity. The argument raged as to whether they were 'interested' in politics or perhaps 'not politically inclined'. In 1890, along with infants, idiots, lunatics and criminals, they were still not allowed to vote. Early in the decade Rose Scott, who was to become a close friend of Barbara, was on her way to becoming the leading light in the women's suffrage movement in Sydney. At the same time, literary life was burgeoning and the *Bulletin* had established itself as a national outlet for the Australian voice. The experiences the new writers were describing were their own, and this gave a feeling of identity and validity that had been slow to come to Australia. The horror of early pioneer life had so affected the immigrants that, at the first chance of release, they'd run headlong back into the reassuring comfort of European traditions and literature. It was an accepted standard to judge things by, easy and proven. The reality of life in outback Australia had become obscured by romantic myth, built to honour the part it had played in the birth and wealth of the nation and to sustain it through its harsh beginnings.

Barbara had no illusions about her experience. She saw the bush as she found it, unbearable in part, beautiful and haunting in others. She had come to terms with it while she had to, but she wasn't going to pretend it was a garden. The gardens in Sydney *were* gardens – the bush was a battleground. The rollicking stories of adventures along the banks of the Condamine were in stark contrast to her own experience. Adding insult to injury, the grinding drudgery associated with working the land was being turned into comedy by some writers, ashamed of its harshness. The selector, battling his way against the seasons, was being neatly written up as a figure of clod-hopping fun for the city reader, and it must have been with a real sense of vindication she sat down to 'write the bush out of her'.

In the beginning it was a cathartic not a literary process, but as she saw other writers publishing their own experiences of the bush in the *Bulletin*, she grew more confident. She began to see that writing would serve the dual purpose of putting her experiences out and away from her and allowing her into a world where she was not judged solely by the social values of the time.

The *Bulletin* was read widely throughout Australia, and she must have realized that there could be no greater revenge than to write up her old antagonists in all their horror. She had made a habit of observation, and she was not so far away from her experience in outback New South Wales that she could not remember the last decade in great detail. She rose before seven every morning to set her thoughts down and try to shape her memories into coherent stories. She did not bother to disguise her victims much, changing names only superficially, from Lennard to Stennard, and Goorianawa to Gooriabba.[3]

Her first story concerned the rape and murder of a young bushwoman alone with her baby in an outback hut. The parallels with her own life in the bush are obvious, backed up by a wealth of detail and a flair for suspense.

In 1896 she submitted the story to A. G. Stephens, who had been literary editor of the *Bulletin* since 1894. He was an awkward man with a nervous, eccentric manner. Norman Lindsay, in his collection of *Bohemians of the Bulletin* described him as distinctly uncomfortable around opulently feminine women. Never an obviously pretty woman, Barbara could not have upset him much in this way, and she made sure by her politeness and almost courtly deference that she did not, but her style of writing suited him well.

He had been criticized for making his 1895 Christmas edition of the *Bulletin* cater for 'unlettered tastes'. In his own defence he said the *Bulletin* 'disseminates a wonderful amount of decent literature for its price, and a very reasonable quantity of art. It was not at all Philistinish and if it were it would not be wholly to blame. For mark this: whilst the neurotic Bohemian refines gross spirits, it is the Philistine who provides the race with healthy bodies'.[4] This attitude was absorbed almost wholesale by Barbara and, by the time she had submitted her first story, she was already deeply influenced by the *Bulletin* and was to become more influenced by Stephens as their collaboration grew.

Whether by coincidence or association, many of Stephens's idiosyncrasies became hers, and it is hard to imagine a man who could have suited her more as a mentor. Initially she appears to have agreed with him on almost every topic, and her attitudes reflected the *Bulletin*'s fairly wholeheartedly until she left Australia. Her closeness to Stephens was based on their mutually complementary weaknesses which combined to create a 'folie a deux' of a friendship that lasted well into the next century and was to be jealously guarded by Barbara.

Miles Franklin had just had her novel *My Brilliant Career* published when Barbara met her in Stephens's office. The novel was a 'bookful of sunlight' to him, and he had given her a large box of chocolates as a token of his appreciation. Miles Franklin still had the box on her lap when she and Barbara sat together waiting for the tram, Miles chattering in her excitement at the success her book was having. There was no response. After a few minutes Miles began to notice how sallow Barbara's skin was and how untidy her hair. Then Barbara smiled rather sardonically and Miles was left with the distinct impression she had sounded foolish. Barbara was envious. Talented and published girls of eighteen were not the sort of people she wanted to spend a lot of time with.[5] She had learnt to distrust girls of eighteen, no matter how 'fresh, natural and sincere' Stephens thought them.

In 1896 Stephens published Barbara's first story, which was bleak and not at all designed to lighten gross philistine spirits. In 'The Tramp'[6] Barbara described how a young woman, left alone with her baby in an outback house, makes every effort to fob off and then shut out a passing swagman. In her attempts to protect herself she had pretended her husband was sick and 'had gone in from the kitchen to the bedroom, and asked questions and replied to them in the best man's voice she could assume.' But he had not been deceived and later that night she placed her mother's big brooch and some food on the table as a bribe and crept to bed with her baby. She was woken later in the night. 'What woke her? The wonder was that she had slept – she had not meant to. But she was young, very young. Perhaps the shrinking of the galvanized roof –

hardly though, since that was so usual. Yet something had set her heart beating wildly.'

The man tries every way to get into the house. She can see him through the cracks in the wall, moving along the verandah in the moonlight. She holds her baby closely to prevent it crying and remembers the large knife she saw him carrying. Having tried the door he finds a piece of shrunken board that has been propped in place with wooden supports and begins to work at it with his knife. The noise stops. She listens and, in the distance, she hears the sound of hoofbeats. She waits until they are very near and then, flinging back the bolts on the door, runs out into the bush for help.

The house and the description of the husband who leaves the woman for his shearing shed 15 miles away are memories of Barbara's first marriage. The Frater children she taught at Merrylong could pick out many of her characters by name as they appeared in her stories and it seems, by the overwhelming number of similarities, that they were heavily autobiographical. As this was the first story she wrote, it was probably the theme that obsessed her most. She had certainly been left alone many times and most swagmen were, unlike the popular myth, bullying and unsavoury vagrants who spared no pity for the helpless or the unprotected. Like the crows and the dingoes, they treated weakness as an invitation to exploitation. Although the death of her heroine makes it of necessity a fiction, the themes of pursuit and helplessness appear again and again in Barbara's work, and the situation was very like her own had been. It seems likely that she blended her own experience with stories she had heard of other women in the neighbourhood.

In her stories she drew parallels between the human condition and the sheep, binding the two to accentuate the drama. She uses the helplessness of the sheep, the inevitability of their slaughter, and their meekness to link her subjects to the environment. In the care of their lambs, the limpid eyes 'materialized from an atmosphere of sighs',[7] the exposed arch of the soft throat stretched back for slaughter, Barbara saw her own condition.

Barbara appreciated strength, but saw it in herself as a result of trials overcome. She liked overtly masculine men but was precise in her observation of them, having suffered so much at the hands of her first husband. She wanted strength to be genuine and not confined to cheap victories over weaker things. Her fury was intense when she saw examples of callousness and inhumanity. Now she was married to a man who genuinely cared for her, her earlier treatment began to appear more clearly horrific. The defence of the helpless became the backbone of her vacillating religious feelings, and when she came across the stentorian command 'He made ye, and ye have compassion on one another' in the Koran, she was entranced by the grandeur of the statement. Barbara's personal God, always impatient of tawdry sentiment and weak-minded hopefulness, had been growing angrier and angrier with the years. While she dutifully followed Dr Baynton's religious routine, there was a part of her that was not affected by ceremonies that had so little passion. A magnificent and angry Deity was another matter.

In 'The Tramp' Barbara treated organized religion with contempt. She described how a boundary rider, cantering through the bush at night, thinks the figure running after him is a vision of the Virgin Mary and, putting spurs to his horse, leaves the girl to her attacker. The rider hurries off to his priest irradiated by a sense of spiritual rectitude, but the worldly priest, breaking straight through the rapturous recital with an oath: 'Great God! ... and you did not stop to save her! Do you not know?', tells him of the murder that had taken place the night before.

The story is horrific in its implications. It shows a figure, stripped finally of everything except her child. Her husband neither wants nor cares for her, sneering at her sexuality and her fears of being alone. Here, Barbara has written as savage a portrait of Alex as she could, and when later she was to say she wanted to be remembered as a writer, it must also have included the wish that her sense of outrage be perpetuated and not washed away in a sea of domestic events. With this story she had pinned Alex Frater to the wall, like a butterfly collector, neatly and publicly for the world to see, and the world of the *Bulletin*, especially the Christmas issue, was a wide one. That Christmas, secure with her new husband and her children,

Barbara must have felt as close a sense of total victory as it is possible to have.

She wrote to A. G. Stephens several times before publication, offering 'What the Curlews Cried' as a title and agreeing with his opinions on editing, adding that she had limited experience of revision, and no suggestions concerning proofs. Finally she wrote: 'Thanks for the cheque. I enclose signed receipt and must add that in my opinion the honor the *Bulletin* has conferred on me in accepting my story is more than sufficient.'[8]

Alex continued to dominate her thoughts, sitting, as she imagined, blistering under a continual drought, dreaming of his children a thousand miles away in the verdant paradise he believed they now inhabited. Responding to a general appeal for poetry issued in the *Bulletin*, Barbara wrote 'A Noon, an Eve, a Night' early in 1897, full of reference to barren lonely plains and burning sands 'that knew not any rain'. But she was to write poetry only at moments of great almost gothic emotion in her life and would not write another poem for two years.

Over the next six years she polished and revised a series of 'studies' of the bush again and again, following Stephens's advice of 1896, when he had printed a clear guide as to what he considered a writer's duty to be:

The book written in twenty-eight days is forgotten in twenty-eight days: the book that lives is the book that costs a life and takes a life-time. We want an Australian author to spend, like Flaubert, years in meditation before spending years in execution; the local writer, so far, is too hasty, too scrappy; he will not take a large canvas and ample time – or a small canvas and ample time – and create a masterpiece. One seems to see here and there the minds to do memorable things; but where are the zeal, the persistence, the capacity to 'toil terribly' to a far-off goal?'[9]

Part of the goal was to produce '*human* stories ... in which you, the reader, might be the actor'. The end result would be to 'cast a steady radiance over an eternity of time'.

That was an appealing thought. As she said of herself that egotism was innate, to cast a steady radiance over an eternity of time was no mean ambition. Unlike many of her contemporaries,

Barbara did not have to earn her living and could afford to 'toil terribly' in comfort. The singular drive behind her writing was that it should endure; she had the means, now Stephens had shown her the method.

In keeping with the drive to identify Australia as precisely as possible and to establish a literature 'of' Australia rather than about it, Barbara began to copy the accents she had heard. At the time there was great fascination in the literary world with regional Australian accents, and Barbara faithfully wrote down every dropped consonant and altered vowel. This created awkward passages that might have been made smoother if the dialect had been suggested rather than reproduced. An extract from 'Bush Church' reads:

'"Oh indeed," 'e sez, "very 'appy ter make yer acquaintance, Mr Stennard, Esquire," 'e sez.

'"Never mind no blarsted acquaintance," I sez, "w'en are yer goin' ter take yer flamin' jumbucks orf my lan'!" I sez.

'"Your lan'," 'e sez, "I didn' know you 'ad any lan' about 'ere," 'e sez.

'"Oh, didn' yer," I sez, "you ner ther bloody white-livered lan' agent won't frighten me orf," I sez, "gammonin' I'm on er reserve," sez I; "I've paid me deposit, an' I've been ter Sydney," I sez; "I put me name ter a cheque," sez I, "an' ---" '[10]

When Barbara's work was published overseas, this was to prove an obstacle to readers who found the dialect so confusing they felt they were reading another language. Still, she was hoping to convey an accurate picture and to stop the flood of hazy images that were perpetuated overseas. Henry Parkes, writing on English press opinions of Australia in 1861, had been excited to 'laughter where he might otherwise be inclined to weep' by an English lecturer illustrating 'the blessings of cheap tea by quoting the case of Australia. There, he said, tea was untaxed, and "the shepherds on the Australian prairies drank it by the bucketful".'[11] There were no shepherds on Barbara's prairies drinking their tea by the bucketful, and A. G. Stephens did not correct her.

During the 1890s Barbara met Rose Scott, whose house in

Jersey Road, Woollahra, no more than a few minutes walk from Dr Baynton's, had become 'the nearest approach to a salon that Sydney knew'. She was an active, friendly woman of independent means whose intellectuality and gentle manner attracted a wide circle of artists, politicians and writers to her regular 'evenings' at home. And she was an effective campaigner. One of her major achievements was the Early Closing Act which, after years of meetings and negotiations, was finally drawn up on a rosewood table in her sitting room and passed in the New South Wales Parliament in 1899. Throughout all this she took great pleasure in her dress – Miles Franklin commented that her bonnets were the delight of Sydney.

After Barbara's separation from Alex, her image of herself as female had crumbled. Despite the fact that she had not instigated the move, the qualities she had used to move past it were labelled mannish and hard. Even today, one hundred years later, in the district in which Barbara spent her early married life, Sarah is regarded as natural, sweet and gentle, a heroine, and Barbara a 'go-getter, an unpleasant woman'. How much worse it must have been at the time and how it must have increased her longing to be considered feminine, whilst acknowledging the qualities of intellect and endurance she knew she had. Rose Scott's activities were condoned by powerful and significant figures of the time; Alfred Deakin, a future prime minister, once commented that he valued her approval because she was a woman who could think and act for herself without ceasing to be womanly.[12] This was exactly the sort of affirmation Barbara needed. Rose Scott provided an ideal model and, unlike Barbara, her belief in the ultimate triumph of justice was fundamental. Barbara's own figure of justice was not only always blind but also bound hand and foot. In all her stories the sensitive and methodical are always threatened; her avenging weapon was only her ability to survive with all images intact. Under the influence first of Dr Baynton and then Rose Scott, Barbara, with so many unavenged furies in her and so many crimes unpunished, was beginning to think her wrongs could be righted.

There were differences in the ways Barbara and Rose

handled people. Rose Scott had the 'wonderful gift of allowing people to express themselves without reserve';[13] no doubt that was what had led Barbara to her, but Barbara had been brought up in such a tough school that it was harder for her to keep her opinions to herself now that she had the freedom to express them. Years of listening to the beautiful English in the Bible, reading the classics and verbal skirmishings within the family had made her absolute mistress of the English language and she could use her words with a pouncing accuracy. Her hearing, sharpened perhaps by weak eyesight, was acute, and she had a flair for imitation, which she used suddenly and with devastating effect. People loved and hated her for it. She kept her temper under control while she was married to Dr Baynton and moderated her behaviour considerably, but the strength of her character had already been formed. Had her experiences not made her nature into something more steely her sense of fun might have been lighter – her laughter was musical and infectious. But the two women, one serene and uplifted, the other 'with very little belief in anything when in one of her moods that resembled a mind enveloped in dark and sombre clouds',[14] became friends and remained so for the next twenty years.

Around this time, in the late 1890s, Barbara began to take an active interest in the world outside her own and a more journalistic attitude to the conditions in it. With Rose Scott's example before her, she began to allow her wrongs to be righted. The first step was to express an opinion publicly. In an article briskly signed 'B.B. to the *Bulletin*', she defended the right of a trades paper to use George Lambert's painting of the black soil plains as part of its Christmas supplement, announcing that it was not a 'great picture only a good picture, clever and faulty'.[15] The scene was one she would have known very well – black soil plains reached right to the doorstep of the schoolroom at Merrylong – but it may have been something to do with the attitude to education and its virtue, expressed in a letter to the *Bulletin* the week before, that sparked her indignation:

Well, if I were Shakespeare, I would be quite content to be given away with a pound of tea. Shakespeare would improve the tea; and the tea wouldn't hurt Shakespeare. There's nothing degrading in being an ironmonger: an honest ironmonger is as good in his way as an honest artist. As Lambert's work is Australian, and good, the artist should be glad to let it be known everywhere. Why shouldn't the common bush person enjoy it in reproduction if he can't see it in original? 'Ironmonger's puff!' If the *Bulletin* had issued the picture as a journalist's puff, would Lambert have howled? How is a journalist better than an ironmonger, abstractly?[16]

In placing trades on an absolute par with the arts, Barbara was reflecting a particularly Australian attitude. A typical piece of doggerel of the time sneered, 'Jin'yus! Jin'yus! Tak' care o' your carkus!' – a piece of advice she took singularly to heart. In Barbara's opinion, there were degrees of excellence within the arts, but artists and educators were in no way to consider themselves above the rest. She was herself a shining example of the virtue of pragmatism, and she never cultivated the artistry within herself at the expense of the material. Her shoring up of her own personal finances was a defence against an outside world she had found brutal and incomprehensible; her love of antiques a safe and respectable way she could express her personality – with the added attraction of being slightly ostentatious and yet financially sound.

Throughout this, her marriage did not provide a placid background to her activities. Several times during the 1890s Dr Baynton had seemed to be ill enough to die, and Barbara was severely shaken by the experience. He had a weak heart and his condition grew more alarming every year.

Twelve

One of Barbara's stories, 'A Dreamer', dealt with the relationship between mother and daughter, describing the journey of a young woman travelling home to visit her sick mother in a small country town. The woman is pregnant and filled with indecision as a storm breaks over the town and she has to decide whether to jeopardize her baby's safety to reach her mother, or return. But the call home is clear and insistent and she crosses the flooded stream, risking her life to reach her mother's tiny house. After a struggle she reaches the other side to find the house full of frightened, whispering relations and her mother dead. There is a sense of guilt in the story and a feeling of love unexpressed.

In 1898 Barbara's mother, Elizabeth Lawrence, had died, and it seems likely that Barbara was pregnant at the time. The story implies an absence of some time from her mother. It is hard to say whether the journey is an imagined one, created out of a feeling of guilt, or if it is real. If Elizabeth was still at her house in Scone, the way towards it would have meant crossing a creek, just as Barbara describes it in the story, and arriving at the rear of the house to find the disturbing signs of neglect and the hostile dog. But Elizabeth's death certificate indicates she died in Murrurundi some miles away, and perhaps 'A Dreamer' was an attempt to recreate events as Barbara would have preferred them to have happened. She described the path to the house lovingly and in great detail, spurring her character through the dark and the rain with the knowledge that 'it was the house of her girlhood, and she knew every inch of the way ... What mattered the lonely darkness, when it led to mother?'[1] Barbara was absolving herself and pouring most of her ambiguous feelings of guilt over her absence from her mother before her death and her love for her own unborn child into this last tribute to Elizabeth.

The child Barbara was carrying so carefully died. She was in her forties and it was doubtful, given the age of her husband, that she would ever have another. A poem entitled 'Baby' records her feelings at the death of her son:

> My little baby, so brown and warm,
>   Ah, sweet brown baby!
> I kissed; I loved; yet thought it meet
>   To shade my baby.
> I kissed – but not the sun: its cheek
> Soon whitened – ah, it could not speak!
> Its dark eyes void, and ... A woman weak
>   Crys 'Baby!'
>
> A lily white has dropped its head;
> And just as white on its little bed,
> White as the lily, and cold, and dead,
>   Lies Baby.[2]

Two other poems published in late 1899 give some insight into Barbara's emotional state at the time. 'Day Birth' describes the rising flood of optimism that dawn brings, putting the conquest of despair in terms of a battle. A woman stands alone on a beach head watching the night pull out of the sky and feeling the dew begin to fall. As the rising breeze stirs smoke from a small fire into the trees, she breaks through her gloom and smiles – the sun has risen.

Barbara's poetry is the only hint we have of her emotions and this theme occurs again. Strained relations with her children made her cautious of her marriage to Dr Baynton. She was perhaps beginning to realize fully what his death would mean to her. That mind 'enveloped in dark and sombre clouds'[3] was fighting a continual battle to dispel them. Alec had by now become so fond of his stepfather that she describes him as 'first mine then thine' in the poem 'To-morrow', published in the same year:

To-morrow?
Nay, I shall not fear – this is to-night –
   Nor sorrow.
Beside thee kneels thy son – first mine, then thine.
Amid the gloom thy face gleams white,
   Nor need we light
If thou but open thine eyes – so shall mine shine.
Thy lips shew not where, moaning, mine have pressed.
The arms that folded lie upon thy breast
Stretch forth, Beloved! for thou are not dead ...
Yet still, so still! Thy restless head
Furrowed the pillow ere but one hour sped.
Beloved! ever didst thou love the night ...
Sleep on! I will not sorrow –
This is to-night – nor fear to-morrow.[4]

Life at the Baynton household in the last year of the century was a bleak experience at times. Dr Baynton was a deeply religious man and the effects of his Protestantism had filtered into his personality with a vengeance. He was strict and puritanical, an ascetic who was determined to beat good manners and discipline into his charges for their souls' sake. He had little success with Robert, the younger boy, who gave him a wide berth, but then he had provoked the old man severely.

Of all her children, this younger boy was the greatest problem. Robert was only seven at the time of Barbara's marriage to Dr Baynton, but as he matured he grew into an athletic young man with all his father's appeal, so well co-ordinated physically that he could tackle any sport, and with a sense of adventure that charmed everybody – except his mother.

As an adolescent he had several times been out at night visiting girls, making an arrangement with Alec to let him in when he threw a few pebbles up against their bedroom window. One night the noise had not woken his brother, so he tried to climb back in using the garden ladder. A suspicious neighbour called the police and Dr Baynton answered his door to two officers escorting Robert in the early dawn light. In the beating that ensued Penelope went to her room and wedged a pillow under the door to block out the noise.

Penelope had a much easier time. She was Dr Baynton's favourite and he spared her the harsher punishments endured by her brothers. Nonetheless the boys never blamed her – on the contrary, they adored their sister. As well as dark, almost oriental, good looks and a tiny doll-like figure, she had the light-hearted breeziness of an assured favourite. To these deeply physical men she was 'the Ideal'.[5] For the elder boy, Alec, the affection lasted throughout his life, ruining subsequent relationships, and he gladly took beatings for things she had done, considering it his right and privilege to do so.

Carefully disguising her own boisterousness, Penelope behaved like the heir-apparent, hearing no evil and seeing no evil. At school she may not have been doing so well. She was going to a private school nearby and part of *Human Toll*, Barbara's only novel, may have been based on Barbara's observations of her daughter's progress:

Even in the first little school every lesson subject but reading baffled Ursula, and it was so in this more pretentious establishment. Arithmetic, geography, grammar – strive as ardently as she could, the girl could not get an enlightening glimmer even into their elementary principles. With music, unless she knew the tune, the teacher's efforts were wasted. But on wet days, when the attendance of day scholars was few and the lessons were confined to poetry and history, save for dates, then Ursula shone; and though aided by the ruler she could not draw a straight line, her colour sense was wonderful. Teachers are never students of the scholars, and none of Ursula's gifts were calculated to score in that absolute, but unfortunately not obsolete institution, examinations. Disheartened by continual failure, gradually she made no effort to improve, consoling herself when she reflected on the peculiar protégés that Nature selected, for from the mistress downward these learned spinsters had little of what was lovely to the girl.[6]

While this may have been acceptable for her daughter, the same did not apply to her sons. Men had to equip themselves to support their inevitable families. Barbara was going to make sure the next in line did not follow in their father's footsteps.

Alec, as the eldest, bore the brunt of this drive for improvement. Between them, Dr Baynton and Barbara were going to see that these boys acquired an education, no matter what their preference or how strong their father's nature was in them. Near the turn of the century, when Alec would have been seventeen or eighteen, he won a scholarship to Sydney University. Exuberant at hearing the news he leapt onto his bed, bounced straight up, hit his head on the low ceiling and knocked himself out cold. When he came to, instead of receiving congratulations, an argument began as to what course he should take. He wanted to study law, but Dr Baynton insisted on medicine, which had been a Baynton tradition and the condition of his own inheritance. In the uproar that ensued, Alec packed his bags and left the house.

Though Dr Baynton cuts a fine figure as a wicked stepfather at this point, in fact Alec and Penelope were extremely fond of him. According to the dictates of his time, a good churchman beat the 'devil' out of children; he did it with no malice and they seemed to bear him no grudge. Thomas Baynton had given their mother security and a place in life and they believed she deserved it, but life at home was deadly.

On Sundays the household was ruled by a succession of dreary restrictions. No drink except water; no reading except the Bible; no socializing; and nothing hot to eat. The family went to church in the morning, came home, did their Bible study, and had cold meat for lunch. In the afternoon, the adults retired to their room for a rest and the house became like a mausoleum.

As a reaction to all this, Alec went gallivanting up and down the north coast of New South Wales on a jubilant spree away from Dr Baynton. After a prolonged dose of gambling and drinking, he returned to Sydney exhausted. Barbara opened the door and let him in without a word. If his father's character had come out for a brief spell it had fluttered and exhausted itself, and Barbara was pleased to see him back; perhaps she was even in awe of the wildness that had exerted itself. For his part, Alec was now well under the spell of both his mother and his sister, and watchfully appreciative of Dr Baynton.[7]

As if trouble with one son was not enough, Robert now announced he was going to war. This caused a sensation in the house. Only fourteen herself, Penelope refused to consider the possibility that Robert should be allowed to join up at sixteen. But he had had enough of his life at home; he longed to travel and be independent, and the Boer War seemed to provide the ideal opportunity to get away. Like many young men of the time, he regarded it as a chance to see the world and 'do his duty' by the Empire. The Australian states regarded themselves as loyal and reliable allies of Britain. Thousands volunteered, and the men found themselves steaming away from Melbourne, Sydney or the bush, leaving families, friends and responsibilities of all kinds. In 1890 Rudyard Kipling wrote: 'Four things greater than all things are, – /Women and Horses and Power and War',[8] sentiments echoed by most of the volunteers and a suitable motto to explain their actions. Robert was after horses and war and, armed with his father's charm, he was soon to find women, but power was only ever to be his mother's and whatever daring he engaged in, he never came close to impressing her. Looking at his career as a sportsman and mercenary, it would be ridiculous to say he spent his life trying to impress Barbara, but it must have affected him to have his every exploit greeted with such grim indifference.

In 1900 Robert left for the war nonetheless, sailing away to a lifetime of adventure. In the poem 'The Absent-Minded Beggar', Rudyard Kipling describes what must have been the situation of many young men of the time:

> He's an absent-minded beggar, and his weaknesses are great –
> But we and Paul must take him as we find him –
> He is out on active service, wiping something off a slate –
> And he's left a lot of little things behind him!

At home, there was no explanation that would satisfy Penelope. Barbara had let her son go for the sole purpose of maintaining peace in the house, and it was obvious to Penelope that the fact that Robert could be killed in the process was regarded as his own business. She took the first in a series of small mental steps away from Barbara.

In the early years of the twentieth century, through a time of almost continual personal alarms, Barbara continued to work on her stories. She had written enough now to consider publishing them as a collection. A. G. Stephens was a constant visitor to the house. They had talked about the conditions of women and children in the bush and perhaps he had allayed her fears over the inexpertness of her methods: 'Feeling makes the form – the load creates the cart'.[9] It seems he may have advised her not to publish the stories in Australia, for he remarked elsewhere that with all their breadth in some directions, Australian audiences were still parochial and 'stuff far too much respectable "wadding" in [their] ears'.[10] In any case, Barbara had no luck finding a Sydney publisher, but by 1902 she was ready with the final versions of her book of six short stories and, early in that year, she set sail for England.

Three years before she had written a poem, 'Good-bye, Australia!', from the point of view of a young pioneer woman leaving Australia after a succession of harrowing seasons, but it is deeply autobiographical. The memory of her mother, dead eight months before and buried on a hillside in Murrurundi, is recorded as the last strong bond. The feeling is of regret and some tenderness for the land she is leaving:

Good-bye to it all!
God still holds the land, haply;
Still holds me – its toy.

First, our one child died;
And the heart-broken mother
The summer sun slew.

Last flood drowned the stock;
Then the fires took home, fencing . . .
Her garden is gone.

So I will leave it.
The blue waters roll the ship
In the dull, sad bay.

Forget you, loved hearts! ...
This dead wattle holds your dear
Memory ever.

Good-bye to the grave
On the hill; for the far isles
Are calling. Good-bye!

The main purpose of Barbara's visit to England in 1902 was to find a publisher for her collection of six short stories which she called *Bush Studies*. Dr Baynton gave her introductions to contacts that included Lord Salisbury, and membership to several London clubs, but apart from this he had few literary connections in London, and Barbara was left to find a publisher herself.[1] Despite the enthusiasm of A. G. Stephens, it was not an encouraging prospect and on disembarkation she was slightly overwhelmed. In a letter written to Nellie Melba in 1907 she described her reaction:

Five years ago I came to London, and as with all Australians, my fear of the unknown evil of this great city was my dominant feeling. Then on my first Saturday night I went to hear you sing, and you stirred some depth in me that made me oblivious to all personal danger – even to the fact that at the close of the performance I had got separated from my two companions; for I was alone in the opera house waiting, hoping for you to come back once more. One of my friends had the latchkey, the other had my purse; yet when I gradually realized the position, I was utterly indifferent. Nothing mattered since I heard you sing. I gave my cabman a ring and told him to call in the morning. Then, as I could not make anyone hear, I went down the area steps. Some thoughts are more refreshing than sleep, and these were mine till the dawn came.[2]

It was hardly an auspicious start, to be left sitting on cold steps, unable to rouse her hosts and comforting herself with memories of Melba's voice, but Barbara was determined to succeed, and she set about achieving her ends with vigour. She was now in her late forties, but still slight: a well-dressed, lean woman with a dark appraising stare. Her grandson H. B. Gullett describes her as she would have appeared at this time: 'She was very good looking, an attractive person and a very good and amusing talker, at a time when these attributes were more valued.'³ So, although English society was tightly knit and well-fortified against outsiders, she had more than just her introductions to break the ice. As well, London was full of Australian artists of all kinds – she was not the only one trying to get onto the international scene. She spent her time alternating between her husband's contacts and the new-found colony of Australian expatriate artists, and, as usual, she kept a worldly eye on the life their talents could provide for them in London.

In an undated interview on her return to Australia, probably in 1903, she said:

There is one thing I should like to say: I should like to sound a note of warning to artists and singers about going to London. For artists, especially, it generally means starvation. The shop windows are crowded with paintings for sale at two guineas or three guineas, paintings which, if they were in Australia, would rank the artist as a genius, and would probably be valued at from 50 pounds to 100 pounds. Sometimes an Australian artist gets a picture (skied) in the Academy, or accepted by the Paris Salon, and then his hopes run high; but the pictures invariably come back to the studio unsold, and meanwhile the butcher and the baker are clamouring to be paid, and perhaps the bailiff is in the house! My heart has ached for the miseries endured by these struggling artists, and I have known them and lived amongst them, so that I know what I am talking about. The penman or the penwoman has a better chance in London, and they nearly all do well; but with the artist it is different. London is a delightful place if you have plenty of money, but it is a bad place to be poor in.⁴

But she was not poor. Through her contacts she became an honorary member of three clubs – the Pioneer, the Sandringham and the Vagabond – and the first and last were useful and inspiring to her. In the same interview Barbara said:

The Pioneer Club is a woman's club with a long roll of members, and what struck me most on my first visit was the collection of autograph letters of celebrated women (such as the Brontes, &c.), which were framed and hung in the reading-room. The members have debates once a month. The Sandringham, which is at 38 Dover-street, is more of a social club, and is a very delightful one, indeed. It is in no way striking as regards appointments, &c., but its boast is that money will not get you into it. What I liked most about the Sandringham was its perfect quiet, and its air of home comfort. It has about 600 members, but is not altogether a literary club. The courtesy and refinement of its members are its special charac-teristics. The Vagabond Club was originally exclusively a men's club, but about two years ago women were admitted to membership. Here one meets all the leaders in the literary and artistic world, and the first evening I spent there I simply sat and gasped as the world-known names were announced, and I looked with something like awe at all the celebrities as they arrived. There you may meet Joachim, Mrs Patrick Campbell, Madame Blanche Marchesi, Gros-smith, Ellen Terry, and scores of other equally well-known people. At present the list of members is full to overflow, and there are 270 waiting for admission.

Barbara was given a seat in Westminster Abbey for the coronation of King Edward and presented at court. Some time later she went to Hatfield, the 400-year-old seat of the Cecil family, as a guest of Lord Salisbury who had served in South Africa and visited Australia as a young man. It was probably through her husband's connection with Lord Salisbury that she was presented at court and given a seat at the coronation. Dr Baynton's father had been an original member of the Melbourne Club and would have been in a position to meet visiting dignitaries and give help to a much younger man. On her visit to Hatfield, they spoke of the Boer War and he praised the Australian troops. It was the beginning of the legend of the Australian fighting man and it included her own son Robert who had enlisted as a teenager. Barbara probably now claimed pride in him, even though she had disapproved of what he had done at the time.

Despite her obvious pleasure in the social life her husband's contacts gave her, Barbara's driving concern in London was to get a publisher for her book, and she found it dispiriting work. Some years later she told the story of her frustrations to Vance Palmer. She had 'hawked' her book from one publisher to another and had so many refusals she had thought of putting it on the fire.[5]

She began with a visit to the Society of Authors, 'a body which she had been given to understand aimed to help writers in this way', and she was in no mood to be trifled with. An official who, for all she could see, might have been the society, kept her waiting in an outer office while he had 'absolutely not a soul with him', and when she finally did meet him he told her he would read *one* of the stories on condition she paid a full year's membership fee of twenty guineas. To Barbara, whose natural caution had been heightened by marriage to the careful Dr Baynton, this was wanton waste and, accompanied as it was by a casual disdain for her work, entirely unacceptable. She swept out, without 'further seeking his assistance'.

She next tried the direct approach, and sent her manuscript straight to publishers. It was returned with rude notes, and a precious review from the *Bulletin* she had sent with it lost. She finally sought help from Henry Copeland, the Agent General for New South Wales, who gave her letters of introduction to several London publishers. Again she had a bad response: some sent back pleasant, non-committal notes; others complained the manuscript was not long enough, they could not handle short stories, and so on. A small sum was offered for one story only.[6] She decided to go home. Then, by chance, she met Edward Garnett, a reader for Duckworth & Co.

Whether she met him through social contacts or the literary clubs and societies she had joined, the meeting completely changed the fate of her book. Garnett was a well-respected critic, who had influential friends and a reputation for talent spotting. The long list of writers he had helped included Conrad, Galsworthy and D. H. Lawrence. He read her manuscript and liked it.

If it were not for this she would have left England with the manuscript in her luggage. The alternative to official acceptance was to publish the book herself. For the cautious

Mrs Baynton this would have involved 'absurd sums' and left her to distribute the book, which would have meant months of frustration and effort for a very small circulation, attracting little or no critical attention. And by now Dr Baynton was a constant presence in her mind. Whilst he had not wanted to make the long trip to England, the thought of him in Sydney with Alec and Penelope was a continual reminder that time was precious.

Garnett read the manuscript, said he liked it 'immensely', and submitted it to Duckworth's. She waited for a further seven weeks for the reply. When it came with an acceptance and arrangements for a percentage of the profits, 'Mrs Baynton was the happiest woman in England'.

Her objective achieved, Barbara sailed back to Australia, and, just before Christmas 1902, Bush Studies was published in England and Australia. Although Vance Palmer was to say 'English lack of curiosity about people of their own race who have cut adrift is thick enough to be felt as a *positive force*', the critics of the time found a lot to admire. The book was used by Scottish author R. B. Cunninghame Graham as an example of the virtues of Australian literature in reply to an adverse criticism of the national effort, and he compared it to the early work of Gorky. The darkness and introspection of the Russian and Scandinavian writers had paved the way for Barbara's work, but this had no effect on public acceptance. For a general audience used to the escapism of exotic places, regal settings, mystery and romance, this undiluted essence of outback Australia had little appeal.

Through the Christmas of 1902 she waited for reviews and in the early days of the new year one by one they came through. At home, on 10 January the *Sydney Morning Herald* declared it a 'collection of striking short stories' that appealed forcibly to the imagination. Then an impressive acceptance of her style and content arrived from overseas: 'Singularly faithful and powerful. Not without humour of a pleasant kind. The whole book suggests that the author could produce a big novel masterfully handled. This thin volume is worth a dozen books by more familiar and accepted writers on Australia.'[7] This review from the London *Daily Mail* was her favourite and she would later refer to it as a 'very intelligent review from an Australian point of view'. Other English magazines gave encouraging and perceptive reviews. *Academy and Literature* described *Bush Studies* as

Full of the fine art which interprets as well as presents . . . Stands out honourably from what are too justly called the ranks of fiction . . . This writer has a powerful brain. It is quite clear that Mrs Baynton is fortified and amused by an ironic perception both daring and original.[8]

Literary World described her sketches of bush life as 'clear and incisive. It is a skilful hand which has drawn them' with 'marvellous insight'.[9]

Most reviews remarked on her skill in depicting the people and landscape. The Melbourne *Age* commented that they gave 'the impression of having all been drawn upon the spot . . . by someone who has lived among them'.[10]

The local tastes of each reviewer were reflected in the remarks, the Adelaide *Advertiser* showing discreet distaste in its comments when, in contrast to the London description of her humour as 'pleasant', it commented, 'humour of the grim order is mixed with downright tragedy'.[11] The Glasgow *Herald* stated simply that it was 'vigorous and realistic'.[12]

All this heady praise culminated in A. G. Stephens's review of *Bush Studies* on the Red Page of the *Bulletin* in an essay on realism, in which he gave her absolute praise with one hand and took it away with the other. He praised her force and attention to detail, saying that four of the stories simply 'could not be set down better', but complained of rearrangements and alterations to 'The Chosen Vessel', formerly titled 'The Tramp' (the first of her stories he had published). In the final sentence of his review, having categorized realism into three layers of effectiveness, varying in force from the first through to the most powerful last, he takes away most of his praise of Barbara's work with this single line: 'On the first plane only'.[13]

He believed that the people Barbara presented were from such obscure backgrounds and so infinitely detailed in their characterization that no broader audience could assimilate them. Later in the *Bulletin* he was to complain of the absence of an Australian his public would recognize: 'Is this not a perverse picture of our sunny, light hearted, careless land?'[14]

It is precisely because she chose her characters away from this mould that her writing is so important today. Nevertheless, Stephens's attitude was typical of the time: to feel shame for such a bleak vision being presented overseas – especially when 'overseas' generally meant England, and English audiences were apt to be unimpressed with a world that wasn't their own and wasn't attractive. It was thought that rapid and unpleasant conclusions would be made about Australia as a whole, just when Australia was revelling in its increased stature.

The appreciative audience for Barbara's work fell into two distinct categories: the literary circles of London and Australian regional newspapers that knew first-hand what she was talking about. The Brisbane *Observer* wrote that she 'dug deeper than any Australian writer who had preceded her', and the *Darling Downs Gazette* wrote that 'After all the doggerel which has been from time to time foisted upon us by so-called writers of Australian literature . . . it is indeed refreshing to find one who has such a true and thorough grasp of the mannerisms and lives of some of our bush brothers and sisters.'[15]

Barbara took the London *Daily Mail*'s prediction that she would one day write a 'great' book seriously. In the early years of the twentieth century she was writing all the time, and by February 1903 she had begun a new story, which was to become her novel *Human Toll*, on her life and childhood in New South Wales. By this time, her favourite brother David was head of a large family from his second marriage, and Barbara invited his daughter Essie to stay with her in Sydney to relieve him of some of the financial responsibility. She had around her the perfect combination of small child and her own adolescent daughter to provide her with material for the young heroine, Ursula, in the new novel, but she was still using bush themes in her writing.

Her methods were sketchy and undisciplined and she was ill for some of the time. She could not work steadily. Over-exerted and exhausted, she refused to work to regular hours. 'Sometimes I work hard for a week, and then I grow quite cold about it and can't do anything.'[16] She had had three offers for this book, but she made an agreement with Duckworth's, who had published *Bush Studies*, in acknowledgement of their initial support. She promised to finish it for the next season.

She still consulted A. G. Stephens both about the new contract with her publishers and about her writing, and he continued to visit her at Woollahra Lodge. In September 1903 she wrote to him saying she had been working hard through the winter and had much to show him.

In mid-1903, Barbara made a trip to Brisbane with Penelope, now eighteen, to get away from Sydney's winter and rest. A journalist used the new-fangled telephone to ring Barbara at her room in Lennon's Hotel and ask for an interview. The article that resulted is headed 'The Author of "Bush Studies" – A Visit to Brisbane'.[17] The journalist wrote: 'a notebook and a pencil alighted from a tramcar, entered the hotel, and proceeded upstairs, and into a drawing-room, where a bright, animated, prettily-attired little woman came forward with outstretched, welcoming hand, to greet the visitor.'

Barbara told the interviewer that she had never given any interviews before and was 'rather afraid'. The first question confirmed this fear: 'Where were you born?' At once she skimmed over her early life, in the 'Hunter River district', and went on: 'I never remember a time when I did not mean to write a book. I have lived a good deal in the bush; all my sisters, you know, married squatters, and in my first husband's lifetime I also lived in the bush.' This must have been the story Barbara was telling at the time. She had killed Alex off once again, and glossed over her sisters' marriages to gangers and gardeners. It is significant that she left her brothers, to whom she was much closer, out of this blissfully malicious picture – a picture that was almost the negative of a reality that no longer had a place in her life, and for which she felt none of the ruthless regard for truth that was the hallmark of her work. Quite the opposite. Barbara was now poised halfway between Dr Baynton's world and her past and was much influenced by the grand life she had seen in Britain. It may have been part of her revenge to rewrite her past in a way that made most of the people in it totally unrecognizable, but it was also part of her own survival. If she could distance herself from the characters in her work, they would be seen as figments of her imagination – part of her skill as a writer and not the integral part of her background they had been.

Now completely recovered from her initial shyness, Barbara proceeds skipping along to the flattering reception of *Bush Studies* in London and informs the interviewer she is 'deep in a book at present'. At this point in the interview she introduced her daughter, 'a pretty graceful girl at the age where the book and the river meet', who just happened to have in her hands some photographs of Barbara's drawing-room in Woollahra, carefully taken to include the china collection and the antique furniture. From the detail recorded, either the journalist knew a lot about antiques or the quality of these pieces was carefully pointed out:

'Would you like to see my old china?' The photos were representations of portions of the authoress's pretty drawing-room in her home at Woolahra [*sic*]. One view shows cosy lounge chairs, dainty bric-a-brac, rare old prints on the walls, and a dainty and artistic tout ensemble. Another photo is of a rare and valuable cabinet of the Louis Quatorze period, the three door panels of which are genuine Watteau paintings on porcelain. Another large cabinet contains a valuable collection of old china, including a dinner set of rare 'Worcester', which formerly belonged to Governor Denison; and also a tea set of beautiful 'Crown Derby.'

The journalist ended the article with a review of *Bush Studies*, describing them as 'gruesome' and 'powerful', expressing the fear so common among middle-class Australians:

A danger with such studies as these, as with much of the Australian school, is that they may be taken for a fair presentment of Australian country life, and not, as we know them to be, merely the darker side of it – the lewd, blasphemous, and abandoned swaggies, low-type drovers, and general ne'er-do-weels of out back.

The general impression of Barbara from the interview is of an intelligent, intellectual woman, bright and secure, with a strong sense of outback Australia based on her experiences in a previous marriage. It was all very neatly managed and very successful and it produced a public persona that would make good 'copy'.

On returning to Sydney, the Bayntons made the move to a new house in Ashfield, which was bigger and brighter than Woollahra Lodge and 'one of the show houses of Sydney for interior decoration'.[18] They named it The Magormadine, but it is doubtful if she ever told Dr Baynton the origin of the name. The house could not have been more unlike its predecessor in the remote scrubland of Coonamble, and she must have moved through the rooms with a sense of exultation at the journey she had made. The Magormadine had five bedrooms, three servants' rooms, a coach house and garden. The furnishing of this big establishment meant more trips to the auctioneers and antique shops, as well as the hiring of staff and the arrangement of the garden. Despite her protests, the arrangements must have been a delight to her. She bought watercolours and drawings, rugs imported from Persia, a whole collection of cloisonné bowls and dishes from 'a palace in China', Japanese lacquered screens and Chippendale chairs, and plate and glass and porcelain from all over the world.[19] The furniture and ornaments reflected two deep undercurrents in Barbara's personality: the desire to soften her surroundings and the need for power. Faience plates, Indian dishes, oriental bowls, all decorated in the clear bright untroubled colours of spring, represented nature at its sunniest and best. The monumental gilt and burnish of the Victorian era were there in the massive carved claws on her table, winged griffins, mask faces and cherubs. An upright pianoforte ('a sweet toned instrument') sat in the drawing-room away from the sun pouring through the windows, where Barbara stood one day with Penelope to have a photograph taken.[20]

This house with all its Victorian intricacy must have been a pleasure to her and she was proud enough to want to share it. She invited John Longstaff, a fashionable Australian-born artist who had painted her portrait, to come and stay.

Fourteen

The book Barbara was writing through this hurricane of activity contains the figure of Boshy, a careful steady old bushman whose ambitions for his young friend Ursula fire her imagination and comfort her through her harsh experiences. The figure of an older, kind disciplinarian who sickens from heart disease is drawn in part from Barbara's husband. Dr Baynton provided a pivot around which she could safely revolve without coming to harm and, in his orbit, she maintained a discreet and slighter image. After her marriage to Dr Baynton and her success as a writer, Barbara's personality became more forceful but, even in the last years she was described as a 'pleasant pretty welcoming little woman'.[1]

In *Human Toll* Barbara wrote of the struggles of Ursula Ewart, a young girl in a small country town in Australia, first to cope with the death of her protector, Boshy, and then the loss of the man she loved. Through the novel Barbara deals with the effects of a religious upbringing on children in remote ou back Australia, putting her heroine's trials in biblical terms, which culminate in a vision of Christ and the crucifixion. She outlined in detail the petty society and brutality forced on the township by its harsh environment. She used names and characters from her past again, even going so far as to give one based on John Frater's illegitimate daughter, Fanny, the same name.

Barbara represented the care and affection she had had from Dr Baynton in two separate characters: Boshy and Andrew. Boshy is an old man, a reformed convict who plans Ursula's future, disciplines her mind, and plots for her financial security. Andrew is her contemporary and only friend after Boshy's death; he represents the physical side of love. Boshy's ambition for Ursula centred on her abilities and always he urged her to improve, to concentrate, to make the most of herself. She is aware of never quite keeping up to his expectations. Halfway through the novel, Boshy sickens and she has to conceal the seriousness of his symptoms from him.

By 1903 Dr Baynton had been suffering from heart disease for many years and, in the latter part of the year, his condition grew markedly worse. In her novel Barbara described symptoms of advanced heart disease in great detail and, possibly, her own reactions to the frequent crises in her husband's health:

He would lie back, muttering his plans for her brilliant future, then doze till roused by his falling pipe. She learned to watch and at the right moment catch it, but the dread of its setting fire to him or the surroundings, some time in her absence, used to fill her with sickening fear. Was it this same dread, she wondered, that caused his heart to beat with such violent breathlessness when he woke from his momentary slumbers? and why did he lift his arms above his head so often? To get her breath she had to raise hers even while wondering.[2]

Through the early months of 1904 she fed her husband and nursed him, making light of his increasing debility until, in June, he died. Writing later of Boshy's death in the arms of her heroine she said simply of the two figures that they 'could not distinguish the living from the dead'.

Her elder son, Alec, came down from Brisbane to make the funeral arrangements while Barbara remained in a state of numbness. On the following Monday the announcement of Dr Baynton's death appeared in the personal columns of the *Sydney Morning Herald*, and that same day he was buried in Waverley Cemetery. Although he was eighty-four and his death must have been expected, Barbara railed against it:

With human moan the wind o'erhead
Sobbeth among the trees; but why?
They are not mateless. My love is dead ...
I loved thee and I dared not die.[3]

Above
Elizabeth Lawrence's
house, Scone, New
South Wales, 1879

Left
Barbara Lawrence,
about 1878

Above
Penelope and Alexander Frater on
the verandah at Merrylong,
New South Wales, 1860s

Below
Penelope Frater, Barbara's
mother-in-law

Alex Frater, Barbara's first husband, 1920s

Barbara Baynton, about 1892

Above
The Frater children:
Robert, Penelope,
Alec

Left
Barbara Baynton,
about 1903

Penelope and Barbara Baynton, London, 1908

Tom Roberts's portrait of
Penelope Baynton, from a
newspaper cutting

Henry S. Gullett, about 1916

Viscountess Falkland (holding H. B. Gullett), Penelope Gullett, and Barbara Baynton, in the garden of Ugley, Essex

Barbara Baynton, from a photograph published in the *British–Australasian*, 21 July 1916

PEER'S QUIET WEDDING.

Lord Headley and his bride, Mrs. Barbara J. A. Baynton, photographed after their wedding in a London Registry Office on Friday. The bridegroom's conversion to Mohammedism in 1913, it will be recalled, caused a great sensation.

Above
The Australian Light Horse, perhaps photographed on leave in the grounds of Ugley, Essex. The photograph was kept in Alec Frater's scrapbook

Left
Newspaper clipping of Barbara's marriage to Baron Headley in February 1921

Aghadoe House, Killarney, Ireland

Barbara, Lady Headley, London, about 1921

Barbara, Lady Headley,
London, about 1924

Alec Frater, Barbara's son

Robert Frater, Barbara's son, England

Barbara, Lady Headley,
Melbourne, about 1927

Drawing-room at The Lodge, Melbourne, about 1928

Dining-room at The Lodge, Melbourne, about 1928

The Lodge, Melbourne, about 1928

Barbara was forty-seven, at the peak of her attractiveness and rising successfully to the social and intellectual challenge of her marriage. She was beginning to enjoy the benefits of her position, finally able to handle the social requirements with assurance. Now the man who had given her security and support had gone. Her first reaction was rage. She called her poem 'Mateless' and Dr Baynton had in every way been a friend and proper mate. Through this marriage Barbara had gained everything she needed, as well as the discipline her nature required. She would never have so equal a mate nor would the balance ever be right again.

Nevertheless, once the shock had worn off Barbara began to exert herself even more than before. What her sagging spirits needed was an ultimate challenge, and that was England. She decided to make an absolute break and turn toward a future she had already caught sight of in 1902. She would block out the memories by moving away from everything that reminded her of Dr Baynton. If it was possible to move from a small cottage in the Hunter Valley to the show-house of Ashfield, it was possible to do anything. She could bask in the glory of her book. The previous year *Bush Studies* had come third on a list of interesting books of the year in *Booklover*, after the first volume of the Cambridge Modern History and a translation of the work of the Italian poet D'Annunzio. It was a good excuse to send an inscribed copy to Lord Tennyson, son of Alfred Tennyson, then Governor-General of Australia.

In September 1904 she held a massive sale of all the possessions at Ashfield 'in consequence of her projected departure for England'. Keeping a few things aside for sentiment's sake, she went systematically through the house and sold the lot, including plants, blinds, wheelbarrows and rat-traps. The records of her sale at The Magormadine show how elaborately she had furnished the house. In the catalogues, she mingles her remarks on the origins of the antiques with the names and histories of past owners:

Lot 50
Superb and Very Valuable Dinner Service, Royal Worcester porcelain (formerly the property of Governor Denison), border of bleu-du-roi,

with paintings of garlands of flowers, consisting of eight dishes in graduated sizes, sixteen soup plates, sixteen meat plates, seventeen pudding plates, four vegetable dishes and covers, four sauce tureens and covers, one soup tureen, and one salad bowl, seventy-nine pieces.
Lot 105
Rare Old Bristol Perfume or Snuff Jar (formerly the property of David Garrick), with the monogram 'D.G.' on both sides, surrounded by a wreath and true lover's-knot — an interesting and valuable relic.
Lot 130
Old covered vase of Chinese crackled porcelain (from the collection of the late Hon. Sir Henry Parkes).[4]

On 13 September the entire contents of the house were auctioned for 848 pounds 18 shillings and sevenpence. Six hundred items, including some of the best quality antiques in Australia, had been sold for that price. The estate was not huge, but it had been left *to her*. Dr Baynton had changed his will in 1895, two years after an Act of Parliament had allowed women to inherit property in their own right. It had come to her, 'absolutely for her own absolute use and benefit and free from the debts, control and interference of any husband'. Barbara was made sole beneficiary, Dr Baynton 'giving, devising and bequeathing all his personal estate of whatsoever nature and kind whatsoever'.[5] (Barbara was much taken with the form as well as the content of this statement and would later leave countless notes around her house, 'giving, devising and bequeathing' things to people, changing the names of the beneficiaries as they moved in and out of her favour.)

The sale also meant that the people attached to the house were put out of work. Her cook was a lone woman with a family to support, anxious and upset about her future. She told Barbara she had thought of setting up a sweet shop. Barbara encouraged her – she had been in this position herself and was determined to see this woman succeed. Together they baked trays of sweets, biscuits and cakes for the opening, and when Barbara left Australia in March 1905, the shop was operating.

During this period when Barbara was planning her departure, her personality again begins to harden and define. At a party given by Rose Scott she gave another interview in which she does not allow the social nature of the event to obscure the necessary business of promoting herself or her future work. In an article found in A. G. Stephens's scrapbook, Barbara is described as a woman of 'strong personality and handsome presence' – a totally different impression to the 'bright animated prettily attired little woman' of four months before. The journalist, who is vague enough to misquote the name of Duckworth & Co. as Duck, North, and Co., does not falter on any of the elaborate details of the reception of *Bush Studies* in the overseas press.

In view of Barbara's projected departure for England the need to arrange a suitable background seems to have become more urgent. Once again she rearranged her past slightly. Her mother, Elizabeth Lawrence, became Penelope, but retained the maiden name of Ewart. With this mixture she blended the two strains in her background she thought truly aristocratic. Her father, Robert Kilpatrick, became a Bengal Lancer who had met her mother on the ship coming to Australia. The young woman was newly married to another member of the Ewart family, her cousin John, but he was consumptive and weak from the journey. The dashing Lancer and the bored young wife met, and fell in love. He was found in her cabin, but to save her honour he claimed he was there to steal and was imprisoned on disembarkation. 'Penelope Ewart' waited for him, and the two began a long exile in the bush. Finally her husband died and 'Penelope' and Kilpatrick married. Barbara, born at the end of that period, was the only child born in wedlock. This story gave her a special position in the family that she had never had and a general impression of romance. She rubbed out bits of her past she didn't like and substituted the ones she wanted.

Barbara was taking her daughter to England with her, but in planning her departure she wanted to ensure that her two sons were financially provided for. Dr Baynton had invested in a company that had been set up to take advantage of the increased demand for law books as Australia began to function under its own legal system. It was a wise and shrewd investment: parallel to the nation's rise to independence and prosperity, the Law Book Company grew steadily. At the time of his death Dr Baynton held considerable stock in the business, which he passed on to Barbara, who saw an ideal opportunity for Alec and Robert. She set them up in its Brisbane office, where they could make mistakes and yet hold some measure of authority. They both reacted predictably, according to their natures: Alec moved into a discreet hotel for gentlemen residents, while Robert set up house with a fat, red-headed, hard-drinking lady journalist. With the boys taken care of, Barbara and Penelope set sail for England.[6]

As well as her own future in England, there was now the possibility that her daughter would make a good marriage – the idea intoxicated her. It became important to see that Penelope behaved with great propriety. Remembering the lesson from Merrylong days, when the standards applied to the sons in no way reflected the standards of decency and decorum imposed on the daughters, and aware no doubt that the qualities looked for in young wives might also be applied to brood mares and breeding stock in general, Barbara made a decision along the lines of tradition and self-interest, and tried to force her daughter into a mould she thought most likely to attract an upper class catch. Any doubtful imputation could ruin their future in England. When Penelope returned home late one night, after an afternoon ashore with some friends Barbara slapped her face hard – in front of everyone. Deeply embarrassed by her mother's reaction, Penelope did not forget this incident for decades.[7]

Through the weeks at sea Barbara began to feel the exhilarating effect of long voyages that was to become almost an addiction. Suspended between two worlds she revelled in the care and attention she received as a first-class passenger on a well-fitted ship. She was forty-eight and her life had been full of reverses and violent upheavals. The last few years had been successful but fraught, and she had left behind such a tangle of emotions that only a great challenge could obliterate. In this peaceful, suspended state she would be able to leave her memories behind as she physically left the shore. She carried a sprig of wattle to remember the good, but she feared disembarkation – 'To-morrow' haunted her.

On her arrival in England, Barbara threw herself into the

business of finding a suitable house, meeting people, and establishing contacts. After discussions with her daughter, it was decided that Penelope would go to Paris to study ballet. At twenty she was really too old to start, but she had the ideal physique and no doubt Barbara liked the idea. It's not clear exactly when Penelope went to Paris, but it must have been during this early period in London, when both mother and daughter were trying to plot the course of their lives. Barbara meanwhile settled into a flat at South Hampstead with the intention of getting *Human Toll* finished by Christmas and upgrading her accommodation as soon as possible. But four months later she was in hospital. Though the reason for her hospitalization is never mentioned in the newspaper reports of her illness, it was probably a mixture of exhaustion and the throat ailment that she had had in Sydney in 1903.[8]

Working steadily on the book, dredging up more of her past, scraping through her memories of childhood and casting up old hatreds and grievances had taken its toll. Allied to the uncertainty of her new life, she was now trying to recapture a time so different from the present that it needed all her concentration to set it down. To maintain her standing with her public she had to finish this new book she had talked so much about and she began to feel the pressure – regular notes appeared in the Australian press reporting her movements and the progress of the novel. By October, with winter coming, she had most of the book completed and a new house in Kensington ready to move into, but her health was so bad she was unable to work at all, and the manuscript was sent to Duckworth's as it was. The old throat illness reappeared and she was forced to be completely inactive through Christmas, 1905. By then, Penelope was no longer happy at the ballet school, so Barbara decided to make a trip to Paris to collect her daughter and take her to a winter resort in Switzerland for a holiday. Surrounded by proofs of *Human Toll*, eating yoghurt and resting, she was still only able to work half an hour a week by the end of January, when she wrote to A. G. Stephens, no longer literary editor of the *Bulletin*, exhorting him to find a job in London. Her letter also contained a real plea for Stephens's help. She was still not a practised writer and the effort of producing this book had put her in hospital. All her work had drawn heavily on the past and the strain of reliving these times wore her down. The published novel shows none of the usual tightness of her writing, and it seems unlikely that Stephens was given the time or the opportunity to help her with it. *Human Toll* waited for release without the careful editing and rewriting that *Bush Studies* had undergone over seven long years.

Fifteen

During her stay in Switzerland, Barbara had been surrounded by people from Europe who were also spending the Christmas period in the fashionable resort of Grindelwald. Travelling back to London by train, she met an English couple, Lord and Lady Kinnaird, who were to remain lifelong friends.[1]

Barbara and her daughter, now twenty, must have made an attractive pair. They were both very slender and carried themselves well. They were beautifully dressed and high-spirited, and both had an Australian disregard for convention, which probably made them less formal and unapproachable than other women travelling alone in Europe in 1906.

Through her friendship with the Kinnairds, Barbara began to make a small circle of friends who had high connections in England, such as Lord Falkland, a neighbour of the Kinnairds, and Herbert St John Mildmay, who was gentleman-in-waiting to the king,[2] and so, with this new step up the social scale, she waited for the release of her new book *Human Toll* later in 1906. On the title page she had inscribed the word 'Desormais' – from now on – as if she hoped from this point to move into a brighter world, far away from the memories of the life she had described in its pages. She did not introduce her new friends to her past, and very few of them had any idea that her book was anything other than the product of the imagination of a talented writer, if they read it at all.

English reaction to her saga of the trials and tribulations of Ursula and Boshy can best begin with the opening lines of *The Times* review:

This novel of the Australian bush is a most exhausting book. The dialogue is in a variety of fatiguing dialects; and the narrative style is not only pretentious – with a number of strange verbs like 'gloatingly,' 'conferringly,' which seldom leave an infinitive whole – but often unintelligible. By hard and repeated study we may discover who Boshy, and Baldy, and Nungi, and Queeby, and the rest of them are, and sometimes what they are doing and why; but when we do we don't care.[3]

The London *Daily Chronicle* supposed that 'the climax may be regarded as satisfactory, but to get that it is necessary to wade through well-nigh forty pages descriptive of agonized feelings and bodily sufferings, and we arrive in a state of exhaustion as complete as that of the girl who experienced them.'

The *Tribune* declared itself utterly ignorant of the ' "lingo" of the aborigine' and 'Colonial slangs' and warned readers they would be plunged into a strange, coarse, crude and simple society. In conclusion, it disdained any knowledge of so harsh an environment: 'We hardly know what to make of the story, except that it impresses us as a truthful picture of a life that lies beyond our own experience.'

Amongst this pile of exhausted Englishmen a surprisingly sympathetic critique emerged from an unexpected quarter. The *Pall Mall Gazette*, while acknowledging the cumbersome dialects and harsh environment, praised the author's 'Ibsenish frankness' and the force of her description, ending that it was 'difficult to lay aside the book unfinished', for it was 'so dramatically told that one pities all women who have to face such tremendous risks, and face them alone'.

Back in Australia all the reviews were being assiduously pasted into a scrapbook by her son Alec, with the particularly flattering phrases underlined in ink.

A week after the book was released in London the *British–Australasian* published a review. The magazine kept abreast of Australians living in or visiting London, reported news from home, published passenger lists of the constant traffic on the great ocean liners plying between Australia and Europe, and also included essays, poetry, and an occasional short story. It was edited by the Chomleys, an Australian couple whose names appear in all Barbara's published guest lists. That it was possible to operate such a magazine successfully shows not only how many Australians were in London at that time, but also how seriously they regarded themselves, their nationality and their literature. The review of *Human Toll* was headed by a photograph of Barbara's hands as they appeared on the cover of her novel. She was intensely proud of her tapering fingers, reminiscent of Penelope Frater's delicate aristocratic proportions, and used them as her emblem, poised in an attitude half-cradling, half-offering. The reviewer wrote:

No one who knows the Southern Continent at all well doubts that its real history is being made in the empty mocking vastness of the Bush.
  Those whom the Bush has once wooed remain ever afterwards its life-long lovers. They cannot fail to recognise the grimness of its tragedies, the ghastliness of its failures, and the dreariness of its matter-of-fact life. But these are details that are set at naught by its mystery, its romance, by the magic line of its unearthly beauty, and the unexpectedness of the fascination it wields.

This was backed up by an assessment from her mentor Edward Garnett in the *Bookman* of March 1907, couched in precisely the same clipped and disdainful terms her bad reviews had used:

We can conceive the conventional mind urging two objections to 'Human Toll', saying in effect, '(1), the development of your plot is unskilful; (2) your characters are unpleasant people, and we cannot sympathize with them.' To this it may be replied that commonplace people condemn Dostoievsky's novels on the same grounds, not seeing that the artistic appeal lies in the originality and cunning force of the revelation of human life, granted obvious flaws and excesses in the telling ... But any mental fatigue that may assail the reader who has the wit to concentrate his attention on 'Human Toll', will be compensated for a hundredfold by the strange dominancy of this absolutely original vision ... Only imaginative art of a very rare order could so body forth a scene in the essentials, all superfluities being eliminated ... There is not a line of commonplace in her novel and scarcely a hint of sentiment. The terrible earthiness of human instinct, the underlying egoism of our desires, the determining force of a mean environment, the gauntness and squalidness of decivilised Australian life, are portrayed remorselessly in the figures of half a dozen characters ... It is probable that the art that, metaphorically speaking, sinks the deepest of shafts into the fundamental animalism of our being will be exceedingly unwelcome to the middle-class reader who is always struggling to keep his ideals on the soothing and unreal plane of, say, Burne Jones' 'Love among the Ruins', ... We have said enough here to show that if the art of 'Human Toll' is to be assessed, it must be judged on the artistic plane of the work of Balzac, Maupassant, or Dostoievsky. There is nothing in recent English fiction that is so psychologically remarkable as this book. It is an unequal performance, fragmentary and uncertain in some of its effects, perhaps a little too nebulous and confused here and a little too overstrained there. But it is a work of genius indisputably, disconcertingly sinister, extraordinarily actual.

This article was reprinted wholesale in the Sydney *Daily Telegraph*, and the reaction of reviewers in Australia was similarly positive. Regional newspapers in particular were appreciative, except the *West Australian*, which headed its article with the simple statement: 'Too original'. A review from the *Register* in Adelaide likening her the Brontës is covered with Alec's ink underlinings: 'remarkable power', 'vivid', 'forceful', 'decided skill', but most superlatives were heavily balance by reservations. While praising Barbara's powers of description and forcefulness, the Adelaide reviewer found her work too forceful, 'considering that so much of the dark side of life is displayed'. Other reviewers criticized her exaggerations and occasional mis-spelling. Some felt over-whelmed and appreciated the small touches of gentleness, for they came, as the Brisbane *Courier* put it, 'like the scent of flowers in a charnel house'.

On 24 April 1907 the *Sydney Morning Herald* reviewer, having read the critics, struck back at the cultural cringe:

We cannot, from our own personal experience, locate the portion of Australia which Mrs Baynton has selected for the exercise of her undoubtedly great descriptive power. We should be sorry to do so, indeed, for it is not given to many residents in Australian cities to realise the utterly dreary weariness and the squalid surrounding of the life she depicts. But the truthfulness of the writer is undeniable, and there may be many in Australia who can bear witness to it. After all, the squalor and misery which, in their places, would seem to be regarded as mere matters of daily life, is more than equalled in some parts of Merrie England, and the 'toll' of human misery exacted from an existence is often greater than is described even in this terribly realistic work. It is almost horrible in some of its realism, but it is none-theless attractive, just as is the Chamber of Horrors in a Waxworks. The simile might seem to some overdrawn, but the reader who peruses the work carefully and thoughtfully will not, we fancy, find it so.

The general feeling was that Barbara had shown her talent and should now progress to a more cheerful topic. The standard of review varies widely, with plagiarisms, misquotations and mis-spellings. The English *Liverpool Courier* expressed its dis-approval of the 'Twisted unmusical English' but conceded it was a 'vital fragment of Hot South African reality'. Barbara was referred to as Miss Boynton, and Barnton, and 'Boshy' was reduced to an unappealing Bosny. But the widespread attention had given her a place, and she was an established identity. The comment she liked most came from a short note written by British author Vincent Brown: 'the writing is the literary wonder of the year. It flung life at me with the restless ringing power and glory of spring. Never have I known the fiery passion of the imagination so marvellously expressed. Great God, what a refreshment in the weary land of trifling.'[4]

But the world of trifling and mere confectionery was exactly what Barbara wanted in her life. The vivid little dramas of her early years had been made real and lasting, but now she wanted to leave all horror behind and concentrate on art and society. But she had fought to maintain her sense of self for so long that it was sometimes hard to suffer the 'airy superficialities' of the world she was becoming part of. She had tried not to let her surroundings deaden her sensibilities to her early life, and her book was her insurance that this would not happen. Yet it produced an impression of her as tough and 'mannish', as Vance Palmer had expected her to be.

She was in an ideal position to continue a literary career and the next step would be to bring out a new novel capitalizing on what she had learnt in *Human Toll*, but she was much more conscious of the market now and *Human Toll* had not been a financial success. She did not want to write the melodramas that sold so well and made comfortable livings for other expatriate Australians. She read voraciously and, as her literary taste became more defined, the next step became harder and harder to take. If she wanted a wider public, she would have to tackle gentler subjects and move away from the autobiographical topics she had used before. Both English and Australian critics had wanted more books from her, but on a gentler note – society novels.

She proceeded with her life, considering ideas for another book. If the inspiration for her other work had come from her own experience, then she would begin to live the life she was to write about. She would create for herself a social persona as close to her ambition for herself as she could get. Nellie Melba was an inspirational model. She had already succeeded in many areas Barbara wanted to shine in, and above all she maintained a steady balance between her artistic and her financial affairs.

Taking advantage of a shadow being cast on Melba's brilliance that November by a young singer who was bringing London to its knees in a role traditionally held to be Melba's alone, Barbara wrote a short letter to her, full of drama and an almost childish sense of adventure:

I trust you will soon come back to reign over us aforetime, and bring confusion to those enemies begotten by your greatness.

Some day we may meet. Till then and after, may the God who made you, He of your Scottish forebears, keep you safely. With the love of two you have never seen

Faithfully your admirer

Barbara Baynton[5]

Melba had been away from London for the unfashionable autumn season, and the management of Covent Garden, anticipating financial loss if they allowed the relatively unknown Luisa Tetrazzini her scheduled performances, tried to postpone her appearance. But the young singer stuck to her guns and proceeded to turn the dingy 'off season' into a triumph. The opera was a centre for social as well as musical life and when the leading lights of London society began to realize they were being left out they flocked back to the theatre. As Tetrazzini sang role after role of Melba's to standing ovations a letter of support from the very beginning must eventually have borne fruit. Not that Melba needed support, she had her own unfailing talent and business abilities to rely on.

For Barbara there was now some urgency in attending to her financial affairs. If she wanted to write well, she knew she could not rely on her income as an author. She had her daughter to support and an overwhelming desire to get the very best out of life. There are several theories as to how she began to accumulate her fortune. What she admitted to later was an intense interest in financial dealings brought about by the distress of a close friend, also a widow, whose interests coincided with her own.

With typical Baynton thoroughness, she learnt about the stock market until she could 'read' the lists of figures like a blind woman reading braille. She found people to advise her but she knew enough herself to understand their advice and was still, despite her complete dependence on this money, an absolutely fearless investor. She rode the back of Australia's rise to power through the exploitation of the country's mineral and agricultural wealth in the early 1900s. Within ten years, from the 'competence' left to her by Dr Baynton, she had created for herself an income that amounted annually to the original sum.

She had an enormous amount to gain. To be rich meant having almost every daily domestic job done by other hands. With an income of thousands a year it would be possible to have a standard of living barely within the imagination today, and if it were possible it was desirable to Barbara. She would literally design the world she would live in. She set about London buying and arranging and engineering to meet the people she felt she needed to know.

Australia's wealth, plus the presence in London of world-class expatriate painters, writers, singers and musicians combined to give an impression of bursting vitality – Australians were sought after and lionized. The Great South Land had produced a brilliance in this generation that was undeniable, and they bought with them peculiarities special to Australia. The dazzling blue of the midday skies in Australia painted on canvas produced snorts of derision from European art critics, used to long winters and hours of misty twilight. The peculiar southern light that reflected up from the ground rather than down through canopies of leaves gave an impression of a landscape lit from the inside. It was as foreign as the moon and the colony drew together in its need for support.

Barbara held meetings and small receptions which included some eminent Australian and English families. She had, as usual, replied to a flattering letter written by expatriate Australian writer H. B. Marriott Watson in the *Daily Chronicle* and her guest list now included his wife, and several titled English women as well as the Chomleys. Australian newspapers were asking for bulletins on her activities, but by the Christmas of 1907 she still had nothing planned to follow *Human Toll*.

She decided to return to Australia in the new year and, after carefully sending ahead a photograph of herself and Penelope for publicity purposes, early in 1908 she set sail for Australia again.

Her return in March was noted in the society columns, along with the arrival of several of her Australian friends from London. A reporter from the *Star* waited on the dock in Sydney the day her ship berthed. She told him she intended to stay at the Hotel Australia until she could find a 'quiet nest' where she could work uninterruptedly. She also reminded him of her past achievements one by one and read Vincent Brown's flattering description of her as the 'literary wonder of the year'. This done, she disembarked and travelled up to a large and comfortable hotel in the Blue Mountains, to visit the caves and rest.

Sixteen

In Sydney she picked up the links she had severed three years before. Rose Scott's crusading spirit influenced her once again, and now she turned her attention away from any thought of a flimsy novelette and back to reality. As always she wrote about what she knew and her choice of subject reveals one of the major forces in her life.

A month after Dr Baynton's death in 1904 she had written an article on the Crown Street Women's Hospital in Sydney.[1] Rose Scott's concerns disciplined Barbara's mind to continue to keep in touch with the conditions that had been part of her own early life, in which the bond between mother and child had been one of the few constants. At Crown Street she had been taken around and shown the wards for married and unmarried mothers. Single mothers were regarded as 'fallen' women, and the stigma included every barb society could muster. A failure of morals and a malicious and unnatural carnality were implied; any prospect of marriage dwindled away as church and society combined to make the world waiting for these women and their babies as bleak as possible. The sunniest prospect was to leave the child to be adopted, or if the will failed and there was no financial support, the child could be sent to an orphanage.

She had written about a woman driven almost to madness by this predicament, and she ended the article with a plea for more funds so that the mothers could stay in hospital and recuperate long enough to be able to face the world and keep their children.

Another interest she picked up on her return was a 'hospital for foundlings', which had been set up near her house in Ashfield during the last years of her marriage to Dr Baynton.

It had tried unsuccessfully to get government funding under that dour title until the trustees decided to change the name to the Ashfield Infants Home. It had been near at hand, full of small children, and it sparked her interest, especially as it provided shelter for both mother and child as an alternative to adoption. Now she threw herself into a drive for funding.

While she had been in England another writer about children, Ethel Turner, had kept public interest in the Home alive by writing small articles covering the party held there every year. The two women became friends, despite the enormous difference in their style, age and attitudes.

Only a couple of weeks after her arrival Barbara addressed a meeting of subscribers to the Home. She had watched these children closely enough to be able to write one of her hawkishly observant pieces on them, and knew enough of her own children's idiosyncrasies to raise a laugh; the toll of 'only' eleven dead from an epidemic of gastroenteritis did the rest.

The sight of a small boy going up to a close friend who had been sent to stand in a corner in disgrace and whispering 'I like yer' moved all her feelings that true spiritual greatness lay in this capacity to feel compassion, and she used this incident to illustrate it.

Perhaps it was a sign of the times·that she also needed to defend the Home against the accusation that it was encouraging 'immorality'. She incorporated into her speech a statement of her beliefs:

The ... help given to young women who had fallen was for first offenders, and it was a noble help to humanity. The girls were taught that all the world was not against them ... Natural love for their offspring was awakened in them, and as it grew they became good mothers and good citizens.[2]

The link between mother and child was given primary importance in the natural order of things and became symbolic and powerful.

Barbara believed in the importance of the mothering role very much and also in general household virtues like good cooking and cleanliness – the only difference between herself and the prevailing stuffy right-mindedness on the subject being that she thought women should also be publicly acknowledged for these contributions.[3]

If all these good deeds had given Barbara a heady sense of her own moral superiority, she was brought sharply down to earth by an encounter with her former cook. The shop she had helped to start had gone very well, but Barbara was surprised to find this success attributed to God. She told the woman next time she wanted to open a cake shop she should ask God to do the baking and see what happened.

She turned her attention to her children. She had brought Penelope home with her and the two of them travelled to Brisbane to visit Alec and Robert. Things were developing along predictable lines up there. Two years before, in April 1906, Robert had been written into the Law Book Company records, not as an employee but as a small shareholder working as a journalist on the Brisbane *Daily Mail*. His movements from then on are hard to trace. Like his mother, Robert enjoyed embroidering the truth, but given his physical fitness, coolness and gambler's temperament it is quite possible that many of his stories were true. He had inherited his physical co-ordination and love of gambling from his father, but he also had Barbara's cool observing eye, and the combination was devastating. He became a journalist and later a mercenary and brilliant poker player – a sporting man who lived off his wits. Unlike his father, however, he was able to make money from them. By the time Barbara arrived in Brisbane in 1908, he had established himself as a journalist, and was living with the red-headed woman he had moved in with not long after he arrived in Brisbane. She was rapidly developing signs of alcoholism. The pair had travelled through South Africa together on a story and she had become pregnant. Now he thought the relationship, though not boring (a primary consideration for him), was getting out of hand.

His elder brother, Alec, worked steadily on at the Law Book Company, but without much enthusiasm.[4] They were both still under the spell of their sister who, small, dark and full of enchantment, had become even more exotic to them since she had been to Paris to learn ballet. She spent her time telling them stories of the school, laughing at the severe discipline, mimicking the mannerisms of the French ballet mistresses. Barbara and her twenty-three-year-old daughter made a striking combination, and Barbara was aware of it. She dressed Penelope in the most beautiful clothes for this role – in a shade slightly paler than her own. But while the two of them might have made a deep impression on Alec and Robert while they were in Brisbane, it did not take long for the younger son to recover.

At some point after Barbara left, Robert's domestic life finally became too much for him. The child of his de facto wife was born handicapped and, unable to face the situation, he abandoned her and left the country. According to the story he later told his nephew, he travelled to China and hired himself out as a mercenary to 'various Chinese warlords'. Robert was a good rider and an excellent swordsman, and he would have enjoyed the drama of this life very much, but he was too much like his father, and when Barbara heard of his desertion she never forgave him. The break between them remained a mystifying blot to outsiders. When asked about his virtual exile from her, she would only say 'He knows, he knows' – and he did know. He had done what his father had done.

Late in 1908 Barbara arrived back in London with no new book planned. She concentrated on her journalism and the various causes that preoccupied her. She had put so much into *Human Toll* with so little success that it is doubtful, given the effect the book had had on her health, that she felt like embarking on another. She continued to have an active social life and to pursue a cause that would have been in direct opposition to the thinking of her mentor Rose Scott. She covered large areas of London campaigning vigorously against the suffrage movement. She firmly believed 'unreason' to be a woman's greatest weapon and it would have seemed very unreasonable not to take full advantage of the current distaste for the suffragettes to hold several soirées to launch the new women's Anti-Suffrage League. All her experiences confirmed her opinion that women wanted to work for men and not for women. She studied the relationship between mistress and maid, which she later published in an article entitled 'Indignity of Domestic Service', and she knew how capricious these women in power could be.[5] She had seen how some of her acquaintances treated their servants and used this as an indication of an inherent weakness in the sex. She was living in an age when women saw themselves as rivals for men and so regarded each other with intense suspicion. Barbara herself had suffered at the hands of a woman she had regarded as close, and she had few real female friendships, and those she did have always maintained an uneasy balance. She delighted in being perverse and often openly rude, pointing out people's faults and idiosyncrasies with glee. In Martin Boyd's novel *Brangane* the character of the title was based on Barbara. She torments her friends in a way the author would have had opportunities of witnessing at first hand:

When Brangane found herself bored she would go down to Cromwell Road and have a good row with Daphne.

If Daphne did not begin a political harangue, Brangane would attack her appearance, her clothes, or her furniture.

'My God, Daphne,' she might say, 'I believe you got that dress in the Edgeware Road ten years ago.' ...

'Daphne ... What fun it is to come here and drink your poisonous Indian tea. I don't believe you pay more than two shillings a pound for it.'[6]

As she began to move in more elevated circles, Barbara's ancestry became more and more high-flown every year, until she finally arrived at a connection with royalty. To a friend who was boasting she had kinship with dukes, Barbara exclaimed, 'Dukes! Let me tell you, in my veins flows the blood of Princes.' 'Ah,' said the friend, 'One can see it. One can see it.' Barbara laughed.[7]

She had made some friends amongst the ranks of the people she was courting, including Lord and Lady Kinnaird, who were to remain close friends until her death. They had a magnificent house in Perthshire, Scotland, to which she was invited, and the Scots grandeur of the place appealed to her. There were forty bedrooms at Rossie Priory, Roman mosaics on the floor of the entrance hall, and a collection of paintings that included works by Canaletto, Gainsborough and Romney. The interest that cemented the friendship was the Kinnairds' collection of porcelain, which included early pieces of Sèvres, Meissen, Chelsea and Worcester. Barbara, by this time, was knowledgeable and thorough in her appreciation of china, and had a considerable collection of her own.

The further Barbara had climbed up the social scale and the longer she stayed there the more her personality had changed. Her investments in Broken Hill Pty Ltd had shown an enormous profit, and by 1911 she would have been able to consider herself a very wealthy woman. She began to treat life as a stage on which she could perform – perhaps because the freedom her money gave her made her less cautious, or because she no longer had any direction for her literary work, and she was trying to fill the vacuum. She always managed to keep a coterie of interesting and vital friends around her, but she began to allow herself licence she would not have dreamt of during her life with Dr Baynton. At times she drank too much and assumed a posturing matriarchal air with people she thought she could bully, which included her own friends and family as well as people she employed. The social structure of the times allowed for high-handedness in the upper classes, and at times Barbara took it to its farthest point. But with this came a confusing liberality that was the direct result of her Australian background. By temperament she regarded herself as being on an equal footing with everyone, from high to low, but she could step back and deliver a withering speech when she thought some imaginary line had been crossed. Anger removed any cloud from her mind and she tore into people with a surgeon's precision. The same wit that attracted people to her side and kept them there could turn very sour when she thought she was badly done by, and the results could be devastating. Servants left; her friends weighed up the pros and cons and either adapted to her or drifted away. Her children learned to deal with her in their own individual ways.

Seventeen

By early 1911 Barbara was planning another trip to Australia. She had financial commitments and her friends in Sydney kept in close contact with her. She anticipated another comfortable voyage, but this time on her own; Penelope was staying behind as a guest of the Kinnairds.

Barbara and Penelope had remained as close as ever. They were used to going everywhere together, and Barbara liked it that way. Penelope, now in her mid-twenties, had become very expert at handling her mother. Her position as Barbara's favourite did not always insulate her from her mother's temper, but she maintained her own sense of reality throughout and used it to deal with the increasingly imposing matriarch with tact and occasionally devastating wit. She enjoyed the excitements attached to being Barbara Baynton's daughter. They visited auctions, galleries and antique shops and had dinners out together. They went to the theatre and occasionally to the opera to hear Melba sing. Barbara wore long white gloves above the elbow on these occasions and at the end of the performances lifted her hands, covered in jewellery, well above her head to clap at length.[1] People wondered who the watcher, who the watched.

Barbara hoped that Penelope would one day make a good match. She had ambitions for herself and her daughter and a clear idea of what 'good' meant – a title was good. But Penelope was now old enough to make up her own mind, and she had met an Australian she liked. Barbara was at first unaware of the attraction, and it was just as well. Henry Gullett was not at all what she had in mind. Penelope's marriage to a thirty-three-year-old Australian journalist was out of the question.[2] She put her daughter in the hands of her close friends the Kinnairds and took ship to Australia, to settle her financial affairs so she could continue to live in England. She would also visit her son in Brisbane and, as usual, pick up her connections with the newspapers.

Because she had had no further inspiration for her fiction, she turned her attention back to journalism, and in June 1911 the *Sydney Morning Herald* published a long article she had written on the 'Indignity of Domestic Service'. In stark contrast to her social ambition, she had carefully observed the effects of paid domestic work on the individual and its broader implications. She reported the routine and general life of a servant down to the last detail and used her own experience and imagination to put forward a strong plea for reassessment of the value of this work.

Barbara studied the condition of maids, cooks and general servants, emphasizing the situations that she felt would arouse sympathy. She may have used herself as an example of the 'oft-times exacting mistress', but her strength lay in her perception. She was quite capable of playing the devastating dowager, but equally she remained the girl from the bush who recognized injustice, and still felt it. She sympathized with the movement away from monotonous and underpaid household duties to the better-paid, more independent and sociable work in factories and shops. At the same time she valued cooking and housekeeping and general orderliness greatly and believed the monotony of the work involved should be reflected in the pay and conditions of the people who did it. The eight-hour day had already been won for general work, why not for this vital work at home? While she was carefully putting this argument forward she also alluded to her anti-suffrage campaign.

Barbara was also working on her address for 6 July to the Writers' Union in Sydney. She described the difficulty she had had publishing her first novel and went on to explain the English market for any Australian writers thinking of going there. She went through her own experience in detail and gave her estimate of the income that could be expected from various sorts of literary work:

'You cannot score a popular success with serious matter. And unless you make a popular success you will not sell more than a thousand or fifteen hundred copies.' The other sort sold by the ton, but it had to have plenty about princesses and earls and gilded palaces in it. Marie Corelli, Hall Caine, Mr. and Mrs. C. N. Williamson – these writers had got the mental standpoint of the English people, and by telling them what they wanted to be told scored popular successes. In trying to find the secret of the popular successes of Marie Corelli, R. B. Cunninghame Graham (whom Mrs. Baynton considers about the best writer in English of the present day) had arrived at the conclusion that she simply gilded over what the middle-class English thought, and made her books of that; gilded commonplaces, that was all. Mariott-Watson, who lived in Australia in his early years, had been a great literary success in England, but the better written his books were the worse they paid. To make a commercial success he had to be frankly sensational, as he had been in a few of his later books. The Williamsons and Conan Doyle, who lived in the same neighbourhood, drove in their motor-cars – they made 2000 pounds a year or more out of fiction that was not literature at all.

An Australian writer who was doing remarkably well financially was Albert Dorrington – but it was not legitimate literature. That brought in no big income. The people who made the largest incomes out of literature were the middlemen – the agents – of whom, by the way, Mrs Baynton believed that Mr. Pinker was fairest to the author.

The very best writers, if they were hungry for popular success, had all to come down to the mental calibre of the British public, and its taste for princesses and titles and palaces. The Australian Louise Mack, in writing a serial story for the 'Daily Mail', put this sort of thing into it: 'Where had she left her gold pen, with its heavily jewelled handle?' – and then she proceeded to describe the superb apartments. If Australia possessed ancient castles and moated granges and plenty of dukes the English would want to hear about it; but as it was they didn't care a dump for it. India they would hear about as being more romantic (500 pounds was paid for an Anglo-Indian story of 8000 or 9000 words), but not Australia. So Australian writers were warned not to turn down their bread and butter and seek fame on the other side because they had received a little praise here. Though she was ashamed to say that a great part of the general public here seemed to think that you must have the English hall-mark, and that the Australian was of no value. America, Mrs. Baynton said, showed more desire to hear about Australia than England, and an Australian writer would have a better chance of succeeding there. The American magazines would take what the English publishers rejected as 'peculiar'; and so the Americans encouraged clever writers.

Touching prices: From some of the American magazines you would get 20 pounds for a good short story, as against 4 pounds here. 'Everybody's' paid 5 pounds 5 shillings a thousand words; 'Munsey's,' the same. 'The Smart Set,' 3 pounds 3 shillings. Mr. Marriott-Watson would get 40 pounds for 2500 to 3000 words, but there would be several sets of agents to have a bite out of it, and he would have to wait six months for the money. They badly wanted a writers' union in England. (Applause.) The English newspapers: well, they had 20,000 or 30,000 contributors, and they printed what they liked and paid what they liked. Some of the 'popular' weeklies would give you 5 shillings a column if you would accept it, and ten shillings at Christmas. As to journalistic work: A New South Wales Rhodes scholar got five guineas a week from the 'Daily Mail,' and did two columns of 800 words a day for it. The editor of the 'Daily Express' (an Australian) got 950 pounds a year, and the editor of the 'Daily Mirror' 800 pounds; but then they could not last long at it; these rates, too, were enormous compared with the pay of the rank and file. Unionism was wanted in the literary profession: to force prices up – to make the rich papers pay decent rates for writers' brains. (Applause.) Let shareholders, like herself, receive smaller dividends, and have the men and women who did the work properly paid. Editors should get 3000 pounds a year, and others of the staff in proportion. 'You can claim the last ounce of my strength in support of your Union here,' concluded Mrs. Baynton.[3]

After another author spoke about the problems of writing and publishing in London:

The assembled writers and artists heartily thanked both ladies for their remarks. The moral that Australian writers should stay in their own country and by uniting should make conditions good enough for the best of talent, seemed obvious.

Also in 1911 Arthur Hayes, one of Thomas Baynton's original partners in the Law Book Company, resigned from his position as permanent director of the company and sold his shares. The Hayes brothers had been Barbara's financial advisors since her husband's death, now she bought the shares and registered them in her daughter's name. Barbara maintained control over her parcel of shares, which she occasionally gave away in small lots to her children.

While Barbara was in Australia, Penelope had continued to see Henry Gullett and, on Barbara's return to England, announced her intention to marry him.

Henry Gullett was a calm and determined man, coolly laconic and somewhat older than Penelope. After a successful career as a journalist on the *Sydney Morning Herald*, he had gone down to the dock in 1908 with six gold sovereigns in his pocket to take a boat for England – part of the exodus of talent from Australia during the early 1900s. That night he had started playing poker and at midnight found himself penniless. Seeing his future in tatters around him, he had gone to the next room, wrapped a cold towel around his head, and re-entered the game. By daybreak he had won his money back, and he sailed the next day. His family characteristically followed one of two careers, journalism or farming. The two interests remained, however, whichever career was chosen, and those who chose the land were said to go through life 'Shakespeare in one hand and the plough in the other'. Henry had left Tawstock, the family farm in Victoria, early on and headed into Sydney. Although he received no help in the newspaper business from his relation and namesake Henry Gullett, he had become a successful journalist. Once in England he had decided not to join any newspaper and had managed to make his living as a freelance journalist. His natural interest in agriculture led him all around England and Europe studying comparable methods of farming to report back to Australia. He had made long trips to South America and, as a seasoned traveller, was accustomed to vicissitudes.[4]

Barbara faced him squarely and took great pleasure in pointing out the inadequacies of his suit. He remained unmoved and in 1912 he and Penelope were married in a registry office in London, without the fabulous frills and fanfare that would have surrounded her marriage to someone closer to Barbara's dreams.

Perhaps the sight of this happiness and the fear of losing Penelope upset her. She was now in her mid-fifties and missing her husband. Again her poems reveal her feelings. In 'To-morrow's Song' she saw herself as a bird soaring away from dark skies into spring:

> *And if – away I shall not think –*
> *Nepenthe from the rose I'll drink*
> *The one you loved with velvet tongue,*
> *The one I kissed when you were young.*[5]

Barbara's children were now scattered all over the world; Penelope in England, Alec in Brisbane, and Robert, who had finished with the warlords in China, in Austria. He was, like his father, an excellent horseman and had hired himself out as a mercenary, using his athleticism and years of cricket to sharpen his eye as a swordsman. While he continued his swashbuckling, his elder brother Alec worked steadily on in his office in the Law Book Company in Brisbane, making occasional visits to the branch in New Zealand. As a reward for his steadiness, he was made manager of the Queensland branch, and Barbara promised him a certain sum as an inheritance. Robert's de facto wife was still living in Brisbane and Alec the kindheart kept in constant touch. She was becoming an alcoholic. Robert had completely disclaimed paternity of her child.[6]

Despite her marriage Penelope still saw a lot of her mother while her husband was away travelling. They visited the theatre, opera and vaudeville, and took some pleasure in each other's company. Barbara had bought a house in the country, at Ugley in Essex. Part of the reason for the choice may have been the typically foolish English name, but the house was in fact quite beautiful, with a deep thatched roof and well-kept lawns and gardens. Barbara liked to spend her time away from London watching the change of seasons. After her own bleak experience in the bush, she gloried in the green of the English countryside. Writing to a friend in Melbourne she described the autumn: 'How you would revel in the glory of this land, with its sweet bird singers. Now the autumn is with us, and wherever one looks is a riotous feast of colouring, all hues, from the tender green of those untimely born to those sickening from maturity.'[7]

But if weekends in the country provided a placid alternative to London, the outside world was rumbling and showing signs of making desperate inroads into Barbara's well-regulated life. War with Germany was imminent. Taking ship once more in late 1913 she sailed back to Australia to make final provision for her financial affairs. Full of confidence in her power and financial acumen, she attended board meetings of the Law Book Company in Australia and arranged to be appointed a director. She also arranged for control of the company to be handled from London.

She arrived in Brisbane to see her son and check on the company's business, but as the war news became more and more frightening the prospect of travelling back to England alone made her nervous. Alec was not the sort of man to refuse an appeal to the emotions: he offered to accompany his mother back to London.

To avoid the dangerous European waters, they sailed to the west coast of America and boarded a train to New York. Barbara's behaviour grew even more alarming when stimulated by travel and cossetted by her increasing prosperity. Alec had no control at all over his mother, who appeared to be frightened of nobody.

They travelled the breadth of the country on the train, with Barbara taking notes all the while. She wrote back that she loathed the American habit of chewing gum, 'Bovine, detestable habit'.[8] Everywhere people were chewing and lounging about, and she could find no man she could safely describe as a 'gentleman'. But she had had good reviews of her work from the New York critics and she admired the American openness to new ideas. She advised Alec to make use of his enforced exile to investigate business prospects for the Law Book Company in New York, but by the time the train pulled into New York, relations between mother and son were strained. She had bossed and bullied him and treated him like a small boy. When she gave him some money to buy their passage to England, he went straight downtown and into a bar.

Arriving back at their hotel roaring drunk, he was confronted by a pillar of fury. Barbara was used to this behaviour in her younger son, but not in Alec, and she determined to crush it. They argued for a while, and then – in what he thought was a gesture of supreme defiance – he dug his hands into his trouser pockets, found a few coins, and threw them out of the window with tipsy fervour: *'There. That's* what I think of your *money!'* Listening to the brassy clatter, as the handful of nickels and dimes hit the pavement many floors below, Barbara's face hardened into lines of deep disgust.[9]

By the time she left New York Barbara had at least admitted defeat in one area. She wrote back to Australia 'I chew too', and boarded a ship for the last leg of the journey. She wanted to use these times to write again, but her concentration was disturbed by a passenger next door playing a trombone. Wheedling her way into his cabin she asked to examine the instrument. This done, she moved graciously to the porthole and posted it through.[10]

By the time they reached England, Alec must have been extremely relieved to have this journey over. He would have been more relieved had he known what was in store for the next passengers on their ship. On its return journey the *Lusitania* was sunk by a German submarine with considerable loss of life. The war had finally come.

Eighteen

On his arrival in London Alec, like many of his generation, considered it his duty to enlist as soon as possible. He joined the 28th Battalion of the Territorials and began service.

Robert meanwhile, had passed himself off as an experienced cavalryman and enlisted as an officer in the Austrian army. He was in Sarajevo the day the archduke was shot. He immediately set off in his uniform for the nearest station where he told the stationmaster he wanted himself and his horse railed to the Swiss border. Once there, he rode across the border, sold his horse and went straight to England to enlist.[1]

There was a campaign to gain support for the troops already serving overseas and great hostility towards the apathetic, or those who were seen to be apathetic. As the news from the front got worse and the casualties grew, the status of those not yet involved fell lower and lower. The war to end all wars – the war that would be over in a few months – dragged on. The confidence of the pre-war generation, so secure in its image of itself before the war, would take a savage beating, and all the things Barbara had hoped to enjoy as she moved into British social life began themselves to disintegrate.

In 1913 Penelope had given birth to her first child, a son named Daniel, and he died almost immediately. The couple were at first unable to comprehend their loss and spoke for some time about their boy as if he were alive and still part of the family. Penelope's fragility was an even greater concern when she became pregnant for the second time, but on 16 December 1914 she gave birth to another son, Henry St John Mildmay Baynton Gullett – a strong, healthy boy who never gave the slightest indication of weakness or ill health. There was a brief skirmish over his Christian names when

Barbara decided he must be named after a friend of hers with connections at court and a string of aristocratic family names. By the time Henry Gullett returned from France on leave from the war, his son was half way to being a 'Herbert', but Henry announced flatly that there were no Herberts in the Gullett family and there the matter rested. The tone was thus set in the relationship between Henry Gullett and his mother-in-law. From the first he knew when to draw the line and he did it firmly and with humour.[2]

As the war gathered momentum Barbara began her own war efforts. She went to Red Cross rallies in Hyde Park and, with great confidence in her own verbal skills, delivered a speech. Also on the soapbox that day was an imposing Englishman with handlebar moustaches. He spoke well and with humour – they had a lot in common.[3]

George Allanson-Winn had all the qualities that had been so attractive and so dangerous to Barbara in the past. Like her first husband he was a well co-ordinated and physical man; he had been a boxer and written several books on the art of self-defence. At fifty-nine he was two years older than Barbara and had worked as an engineer in India, building bridges over the Ganges. In 1899 he had married the daughter of the governor of Leh and Jammu province and by 1914 had made a 'sensational conversion to Islam'.[4] After the meeting he took Barbara to tea with his two sons. He began to visit her regularly and brought one day a small christening cup for her grandson inscribed 'From Old England – to young Australia'.[5]

An impression of Barbara at this time comes from a young Australian author living in London. In October 1914 she had been surprised to read an appreciative article about her work in the *Book Monthly*. She wrote to the contributor in a large swirling hand – so big that each page carried only four or five words: 'Who are you that know my work so well? ... Where do you come from? All the time I've been over here I've never had such encouragement. Won't you come and have dinner with me at my club?'[6]

Her admirer, a twenty-year-old Australian, was both terrified and impressed by her impulsive invitation. He was staying in a small room in Bloomsbury and had submitted this article on the off-chance the English journal would publish his piece. He was struggling to live on very little money and now he seriously considered travelling far out of London to post a letter of refusal. He wondered how pleased this woman would be, to find her compliments coming from a twenty-year-old. Finally, he took his fate in his hands and went: 'And I was glad I did, for Barbara Baynton was a large, generous woman, who wasn't at all likely to humiliate a boy. In that fashionable club she still seemed like a bushwoman; there was an atmosphere of abundance about her.'

They talked of literature. She told him she admired the Russian and Scandinavian writers: 'She felt that the human condition in those countries was much the same as in our own; and that their peoples faced the same problems. She admired their starkness and simplicity. Most of the fashionable English writing of the day she regarded as mere confectionery.' The dinner was a success and the friendship lasted, as did the literary career of the young Vance Palmer. Years later he wrote of her:

In essence for all the taste for high life she later acquired, she was a simple woman – gusty, forthright, robust – like Miles Franklin, but with more weight behind her. She had been brought up on the Hunter River when it was a more primitive place than it is now, and her mind was full of vivid little dramas of loneliness and people a little unhinged by isolation. Sometimes her writing rasped the nerves with its sheer violence ... But her conversation had a humor and a devastating wit – as instanced by her nickname, 'Dingo Dell', for a certain Anglo-Australian club haunted by the sort of people who aped English habits and yet couldn't help emphasizing their origins by cooeeing to one another across Regent Street. 'Dingo Dell!' ... She was so fiercely determined to reveal the truth about life, no matter how bitter or brutal it might be. I often wondered if her society friends ever read her sketches.[7]

Barbara had settled back into society on her return to London. She entertained lavishly. The soft and feminine clothes of the day suited her and she chose her materials and colours with great care and subtlety, so that the strength of her features and the resolution in her manner were greatly softened. Her hair was swept up off her face and arranged in curls. She always dressed for dinner and enjoyed the pageantry and formality of it to the fullest. She took great care with her appearance for the evening, had beauticians and maids to help her prepare, and could arrive giving an impression of 'beauty and distinction' that would have pleased her.[8] She began to accumulate an assortment of tiaras and necklaces, brooches and earrings, bracelets and rings that would have suited a prince of the Ottoman Empire.

Meanwhile London society was rousing itself to entertain the troops on leave. In keeping with the time, most matrons were hurrying to invite officers. Barbara, however, decided to open her house exclusively to 'other ranks', and hardened this decision to other Australian ranks only. She and Penelope, who was staying with her while Henry Gullett was in France, went out and around London and brought Australian soldiers home from the park and streets, wherever they recognized the uniform.

Henry Gullett had been beyond the age limit for enlistment at the outbreak of war so he had gone to France as official Australian war correspondent. As a result of what he saw there, he returned to England and went back to France as an ambulance driver. His son Henry Baynton Gullett describes his efforts:

It must have been an horrendous experience for the wounded. He was always a horrid driver. Not horrid but he drove as he rode a horse – with a firm hand. The brakes slightly on in case it should get any foolish ideas – yet he would keep it going with the spurs. He was a great burner out of clutches.

Meanwhile his wife and Barbara were caring for Australian troops in Britain, whether they were on leave from service in Europe or newly arrived from Australia. And little else was done for them at all. They arrived in London and went to the Information Bureau where they were given a bath, a cup of tea and a bun, and charged threepence. From there they wandered round the sights of London, and it was on these walks that they were most likely to come upon an imposing matron and a slim dark young woman making straight for them. In an article published in the *British–Australasian* at the end of the war, Barbara showed her anger at the careless treatment these men received:

When the European soldier gets leave, he goes home to parents, wife, or relations. He, at least, goes home. How often does that apply to our shy wayfarers? What signifies home to them? The deserted Christ in his bitter Gethsemane, was not more desolately lonely than thousands of my countrymen. And while on the saintly subject, I may remark that even that Divine Leader had among his few followers, one black sheep. The Australian soldiers generally speak no foreign tongue. One day he leaves the thunder of guns and shells, and the deadly poison gas. When he leaves these and other atrocities created by the worse than cannibal Huns, and comes for a short respite, say, to London, small wonder that the prowling harlot, even if she speak but broken English and borders on the half-century, finds these boys easy victims.[9]

Though these men might have been surprised to hear themselves referred to as 'shy wayfarers', they must have been pleased to find some warm reception in what was otherwise a fairly indifferent atmosphere. One man, Private Hocking, has recalled his experiences as a young soldier in London:

In 1915 when we arrived, London was an entirely different city than what you know now. In a way it was the centre of the world and there was a tremendous amount of arrogance and self-satisfaction about, and also a feeling of being a 'colonial' – a superiority that they seemed to emanate. The English forces didn't like us at all – they didn't like us at all . . . It was not what you might call 'Homey'.[10]

With only hostels and the occasional night out organized for them, the men were ripe pickings for prostitutes and unscrupulous cabmen, anyone clever enough to relieve them of their pay.

To Barbara it seemed these 'Woolamalooites [*sic*], Rock-pushites, and New South Wales men', as she described them, deserved better. She formed an association called The Australian Wanderers. Through the war she invited 8000 Australians to her houses in London and Essex, and looked after them as best she could. Penelope wrote their letters home and one, Stan, went down in family legend. He was walking with Penelope one day when an officer passed them. Stan continued strolling idly by.

'Stan, that was an officer wasn't it? Aren't you supposed to salute?'

'Ah lady, if I saluted every officer I walked past I'd never have m'hands in m'pockets.'

At her country house in Ugley, Essex, Barbara hired a pony and trap for the men to use around the countryside. They politely stepped into it and tootled down to the pub. Most of them were used to riding bush horses and one, a mountain man, Jack White, politely lied to her when she asked him what he thought of the pony. Years later he would tell her grandson as they drove their stock to the snow leases of the High Country, he thought it 'a nasty, short stepping little bastard', but to her face he had said he liked it.

Barbara wrote that while the soldiers were with her

though they may have stayed a day or a month, not one of these boys ever abused my shelter, nor did an offensive action, nor said an indecent word, and from my heart I testify that no one ever left me after a long or short stay, but that I felt their debtor, for their gratitude, and later on their mothers', has enriched me as long as I live.

Throughout the war she continued to be active on the board of the Law Book Company, using her position to force the vote and alter the articles of association to give total power to only two directors at a time – one of whom she planned to make herself. This done, she enjoyed herself in her capacity as director of the Law Book Company, declaring huge dividends with her new power one day and then, after a hurried overnight consultation with her advisors, returning the next day to readjust to a more moderate sum that would allow for the ordinary running costs. Nonetheless, she was wise enough to take advice and the company continued to show a steady increase in profit.[11]

As news of the terrible casualties at Gallipoli came through, and many of Henry Gullett's relatives enlisted, he began to make definite plans to travel back to Australia and join up. He was offered a commission in the Grenadiers but, though it was a flattering offer, he wanted to be with his own countrymen. In retrospect it was a wise choice. Grenadier casualties were horrific, and he almost certainly would have been killed.

Early in 1916 Penelope and Henry and their small son sailed back to Australia and, despite his age, Henry joined the army. Shortly after he was engaged by Prime Minister Billy Hughes to tour Australia and speak in favour of Hughes's conscription campaign.

For Barbara this was the first trip her daughter had taken away from her which had not been instigated by her. With the knowledge of Penelope's increasing autonomy she buried herself in her writing and the constant stream of visitors. She began working on a new story about an Australian soldier, drawing on her experiences of the soldiers she had met.

Barbara had bought a new house in Great Cumberland Place. It was five storeys high, the bottom forming the kitchens and the top the maids' quarters. There was a staircase with a balustrade round the first floor. She had butler, maids and a Mrs Moon to cook for her. She had pursued her taste for chinoiserie and, in the constant process of trading and upgrading her collection, had ended up with a set of beautiful red lacquer chairs with a large desk and mirror. She wrote daily at this desk, which was decorated with fantastic birds and demure, rigid Chinamen that mirrored the frozen stances of the overfed spaniels and shepherdess figurines in her cabinets. From her interest in Arab and Muslim cultures she had acquired a taste for grandeur and the exotic. The pattern on her curtains was large and barbaric – a huge green vine twisting upwards in rough weave with strange fruit and swirling leaves, on which sat parrots and peacocks and birds of paradise. She bought an enormous mirror, so large it had to be lifted in in sections, which covered the wall and was painted with cupids and dangling floral swathes. It formed a floral border like a halo around whoever stood inside its circumference.

Into all this came a stream of diggers on leave. Barbara managed to dampen the effects of her surroundings by her plain affection and ceaseless questioning about their experiences. She had small mementoes around the sitting-room, a piece of metal from a Turkish sniper's bullet, a fir cone from the Lone Pine. They played cards and she helped them to write letters home, for some were barely literate. If there was time, they stayed in Essex with her and visited the city only for nights out to theatres and music halls at the weekend.

In July 1916, in the summer issue of the *British–Australasian*, Barbara published another story, called 'Trooper Jim Tasman'. Although the name must be fictional, the piece is based on the stories of the men she had already met and it seems, from her specific references, that she based the character on one soldier.

She missed her daughter and these men moved her deeply with the nature of their bravery. Most of them were country men and despite their uncertainties in London, they maintained their essential Australianness. When Trooper Jim was taken down by cabman and charged ten shillings for what he knew was a tenpenny fare, a passerby saw the injustice and took up the quarrel on the soldier's behalf. The cabman was taken to court, fined and his licence suspended, but Jim and his mates took no pleasure in the decision. They brought supplies to the family and paid the cabbie back the fine. This good-heartedness, plus the stark tales of their soldiering were a very appealing combination, and other Australians in London were not immune to it.

There was a core of common homesickness too. Occasionally in the midst of a recital of this incident or that a silence fell:

He lowered his head and wailed a weird, wild tune that wafted me back thousands of miles, and, it seemed, thousands of years. His words were a tribute to never-forgetting 'Australia' and the good 'gurls' left behind. And, as ever, his sentiments were shiningly endorsed by his comrades. Then even Jim's lips closed with a grimness, for we were all spell-bound in the fellowship of loneliness and longing for our own land.

'But your mother said nothing?' I asked again.

'Not a blarny word. Yer see, if she'd made a 'ole in 'er face she'd a' been gone a million; bowled me over meself, p'r'aps, front me cobbers.'

He went on talking, but he had conjured a picture for me of his speechless mother that blotted out all else. I saw those silent bush women. Early pioneers, who had left father and mother, and sister and brother and friends, to face the great unknown as mate to their man, and of their silent courage had bred these Anzac heroes.[12]

She ended her story with an incident with Jim in Claridges. An American had approached the soldier and asked him if he was alone. He had already been taken for almost all his pay while on leave and this stranger disconcerted him. Pointing to Barbara, who was standing some feet away in hat, gloves, feathers and furbelows, he said 'That's me mother', and then 'flushed and embarrassed' hurried over to apologize. She took his arm and, 'so linked, mother and son passed down Brook Street'.

These soldiers were so suited to give her what she needed: the feeling of mothering without the terrible emotional echoes and rebounds that every gesture and word from her own sons set up in her, and in her role of mentor and mother she could have safe contact with the sort of physical and boisterous Australians she had known in her youth. She felt an intense pride and defended their character and essence of Australianism in public and in print. Thousands had passed through her house now – in the course of a year an average of forty a week. Gradually letters began to arrive from their mothers in Australia.

Barbara's sympathy with and interest in these men was in stark contrast to her feelings towards her sons. Both Alec and Robert were wounded at some stage during the war, and, though she used all her contacts to extricate them from the dreadful conditions in the field hospitals, and though once back in England she cared for them until they had recovered, she plainly preferred these other soldiers to her own sons. The exact timing of their recovery with their departure from her house to other lodgings in London was a little too neat.

In Australia the referendum for conscription had been lost, and Henry Gullett, now a sergeant, and his family were sent by troopship to England to prepare for action. On board the *Osterley*, they held parties and games and trained and exercised daily. Henry Gullett edited the ship's magazine. The men called this breezy interim between sanctuary and the unknown 'Osteralia' and, in typical form, a photograph of twelve men in shorts and slouch hats lying flat on their backs in the sun was published in this little magazine under the heading 'Keeping Fit'. They received no pay while on board, and the food was so poor a mock funeral was given to an experimental meal of flying fish, complete with band, procession and a valediction by Father O'Hagan: 'Ashes to Ashes, dust to dust, if the soldiers won't eat you, the fishes must.'[13] Despite the light-heartedness, there were real fears for their safety during the passage, from the German 'tin fish' that harried the convoy.

On arrival in England, Henry was transferred to Salisbury Plain for training, and Penelope and her boy, now with his own nickname, 'Jo', moved to London to stay with Barbara.

The capital was under constant bombardment now and Great Cumberland Place made some faint gestures toward self-protection. Under the well of the big staircase a light black cloth was pinned to form a small alcove. During raids the small boy was hurried into this dark space, which gave an impression of safety if nothing else. In defiance of all rules of self-protection, they all trooped outside to watch the criss-cross of the searchlights in the night sky as they hunted for zeppelins.

By 1917 the war had taken a terrible toll on Australian troops. Many of the boys Barbara had sheltered would not come back and the trail of soldiers in and out of her house left its mark on her. She was a strong woman and resolute in her determination to enjoy her life but in every leavetaking there was the almost certain knowledge that the departing figure would never be seen again. She continued her work for them, but the effect of so many 'going south' was telling.

Barbara's publisher, Duckworth, had decided to reissue *Bush Studies* with two new stories included, and she was busy editing and correcting her original manuscripts as well as polishing and defining the later stories. The book was to open with 'Trooper Jim Tasman' and end with her latest story 'Toohey's Party'. She had had to do without A. G. Stephens's help for some time and took great pains to clarify and correct. *Human Toll* had suffered from its hasty release and perhaps she knew that she had her chance with this edition to present her stories in their final form.

The new edition was published under the title *Cobbers*. Though the story of Trooper Jim which headed the collection, was more a piece of journalism than a well-crafted story, she had many good reasons for putting it first, despite the fact that it sat uneasily ahead of her collection of bush stories.

Sir George Reid, who was a friend of Barbara's and Australia's first High Commissioner in London, wrote a preface to *Cobbers*, which had, as usual, a build up of publicity given to it in the *British–Australasian*. The word 'cobber' was translated for English readers as 'chums', and this perhaps was necessary. An English article had referred to it as *Cobblers*.

The book was prefaced by another poem entitled 'To-morrow'. Her memories seemed to crowd her again. She longed to be set adrift with her companions, with no points of reference, in a suspended state where memory sleeps:

> *To-morrow I'll sail in a shadow-ship*
> *With a phantom obedient band,*
> *Who'll murmur not when past ports we slip,*
> *For we'll never, we'll never land.*

This desire to escape was echoed in Barbara's fascination with sea voyages. On these trips she felt a release from the pressures of her life and a resolution to her dilemma as to her identity. Half way between England and Australia she was neither expatriate nor patriot and she could relax. She used the image of a ship with no destination to convey her desire for release from the sense of grief and despair the war had brought her.

By June 1917 the Australian troops posted on Salisbury Plain had spent long hours parading in bitter weather and were sick and tired of the cold and the pointless activity. Apart from the dull rage on behalf of the men, Henry Gullett had pleurisy and was seriously ill.

The men were bored and restless. Some were making frantic efforts to get into the Air Force, using as a pressing reason the fact that they had read in *The Times* that twenty-three airmen had been killed the week before, and there must therefore be room for them – one of these was Barbara's second son, Robert.

At the height of that summer Barbara published another poem in the *British–Australasian*. Called 'The Broken Bough', it begins with the lines:

> *Too frail seems my shelter for this night*
> *Of wind and storm and subtle fears.*

She described her feelings within the elaborate shell of the material world she had created for herself. It is hard to tell if this bitter poem is written about Dr Baynton or her first husband, but the overwhelming feeling is one of loss and betrayal. Perhaps she cut too short the period of her grief in an attempt to forget it and move forward. She had not allowed herself a gradual process of dissolution and reconstruction after the death of Dr Baynton. Slowly this bitter resolve delineates her character more than her other qualities and the sharp defence of 'self' makes her wit more cruel. The high casualty rate did nothing to lighten her spirits.

Australians were making their way in this war and it was a very particular way and very hard won. Like all Australians of her day she moved with and reacted to the fortunes of her countrymen and perhaps, in the pointless death of so many, felt as if all youth and brightness were dying and the autumn of her own life approaching. She wrote regularly to her son-in-law, whose complete independence had won her respect. She had tried to dominate him and had used the fact that he was seven years older than Penelope to refer to him as 'the old man', but it had not had the belittling effect she had hoped. Close proximity to two of the most difficult Australians of the day – Billy Hughes and Barbara Baynton – each of whom acknowledged the other as troublesome, is testament to his character. He was calmly indifferent to her moods, could beat her in an argument, and was able to handle the crises that marriage to her daughter inevitably brought. He tried, as her ambition for him escalated, to maintain a sense of balance, and she found, to her surprise that, rather than Henry Gullett bending to her will, she was adapting to him.

After a brief summer in England, Henry Gullett was sent to Palestine to cover the campaign as official war historian. He kept in close touch with his family in London, sending his son pictures and mementoes and keeping Barbara up-to-date with the enterprises of the troops. To Penelope, who had moved out of Great Cumberland Place with her son, he wrote of his weariness with 'hoofing it round the Holy Land', but his reports glow with a compassionate understanding of the situation as a whole. By Christmas 1917 he had seen the capture of Jerusalem. Despite the weakness in his lungs that pleurisy had given him, he had reached the city so early in the advance that a soldier, hearing a mechanical clicking in what was thought to be an unoccupied house, had stormed upstairs, gun at the ready, only to find Henry Gullett sitting on an upturned box with his portable typewriter, tapping out his reports as the troops marched in.

He wrote home to Barbara in London, 'I wish you could see our beautiful, wonderful boys … old wine in new bottles, there never will be another Australian Imperial Force. Only a new free country could have bred these heroes.'[14]

In the bitter cold of December in London, the effect of Henry Gullett's experiences in Palestine were to be a permanent influence on Barbara's opinions. She had an instinctive love of splendour and pageantry, all things mystic and powerful. The might of religious experience expressed in cultures other than her own impressed her: it matched her own depth of feeling. Henry Gullett informed and broadened her perception, and sparked her interest in the history of other religions, in particular those of the Muslim world. She despised 'weakminded hopefulness',[15] but was herself deeply superstitious and pinned her own hopes to strange totems. She walked ceremoniously around a particular tree in Hyde Park to invoke good things and touched a large china Buddha for a benediction.[16] They all coincided with a deep mystical core that was never quite set or formed enough to bring her comfort but, for most of these years, the sounding brass and the tinkling cymbals were still enough.

As well as his reports, Henry sent back to his wife and son pressed flowers and pictures and descriptions of Jerusalem and the Holy Land which gave them all that Christmas a greater sense of the reality of the day than ever before.

Into the winter of 1917–18 Barbara continued to entertain and care for the men on leave. During the year, however, the soldier she had represented as 'Trooper Jim Tasman' was killed. She had helped him to learn to write and he had kept in touch with her. 'I notice he has almost discarded the use of the little alphabet; but then one expects capitals from him.' Of his departure she had written, 'Whatever befalls you, my dear countryman, the daring glory and sentimental grace of your courage will shine through my life.'[17]

She still kept open house and maintained contact with the relatives of the men, but they began to appear to her less a group of individuals, and more a crowd. From this point she stopped seeing real faces. 'I purposely have lost count how many now, for so many will come back no more, that I only press forward.'[18]

She was still seeing Lord Headley. Her elder son, Alec, had been courting a young Welshwoman who had looked after him and helped him recover after his time in hospital. A slight, softly spoken young woman, she saw Barbara and Lord Headley laughing together on one of her visits to Barbara's house. To her shocked young mind they appeared to be flirting.

For a while in February 1918 Barbara had considered moving back to Australia, but by mid-summer she was still in London and running the patience of the Law Book Company thin with demands for loans to upgrade her collection. In late August she made a visit to Upper Berkeley Street to the antique shop of Charles Prior. As usual, when the outside world was grim she rearranged and embellished her environment. In three days she made a most impressive list of purchases, from plate and porcelain, to needlework bed hangings and Chippendale chairs.

A month later, in September 1918, her poem 'Rare Banqueters' appeared in the *British–Australasian*. The theme, once again, was death, and as usual the poem is full blown and gothic in its sentiment:

The fruits of my youth lie about me
On the wild, waste earth 'neath my feet.

Disdainful the birds fly above me,
  So that none save the canker-worms eat.

Rare banqueters these, in worm fashion,
  And besheathed in their symbol of flesh,
They feast on my primitive passion –
  And embroider their honeycomb mesh.

Maker, Thy methods baffle mankind,
  For Thou setteth his heart as a cup;
Then willeth the worm – the deaf and blind –
  Shall have sesame *to it – and sup.* [19]

Two months later the war was over.

Nineteen

Ten days before the end of the war, Alec, now thirty-seven, married Lily Thomas, the young Welshwoman he had been seeing for some time. He had been a good soldier, strikingly handsome with a fine war record, but his time in camp hospital had shattered his confidence, not the least because a lice infestation had resulted in a temporary loss of hair.[1] His leave at home did not minister to his mental comfort. Barbara usually laughed at him, making up dismissive nicknames for his regiment, which she considered nondescript. He moved out of Great Cumberland Place as soon as possible.

Robert was thirty-six at the end of the war and still single. He had spent part of the war experimenting with aircraft. He later told his nephew, H. B. Gullett, that he had helped to invent a way in which machine guns could be fired from the nose of the aircraft without obliterating the propeller. He liked Penelope's young son and landed his plane one day on the lawns of Ugley to take him up for a spin. The child, little more than a baby, endured the strangeness of it all until the motors started and the shuddering and roar became too much. He screamed, and his uncle politely taxied back to the house and deposited the boy back in the arms of his mother.[2]

Barbara's treatment of her sons is the least attractive part of her personality. The two men seemed to be neatly divided into components of her first husband's temperament, and with age and maturity she found them easy to dominate. The elder, Alec, was an attractive, gentle man, fond of his mother and demonstrably affectionate, but without Barbara's ambition. Robert was ruthless, but his drive was not balanced by a steadiness that would produce anything worthwhile, and, despite his appeal to women, he had absolutely no sense of responsibility toward them. Barbara had suffered from her first husband's lack of ambition and irresponsibility, and she kept these two mirrors of him at a safe emotional distance. She teased them and played with them. All through their lives they made slow penance for their father. Penelope had, by virtue of her sex and early frailties, made a much closer bond with her mother. Barbara had always kept her daughter with her, and this security had given her a confidence and lightheartedness denied the boys.

Barbara's relationship with her son-in-law, Henry Gullett, had by this time reached an equilibrium which it would maintain for the rest of her life. She was fond of him and at the same time a little afraid, a feeling she tried very hard to conceal. And he was coming home.

Henry Gullett's close association with Billy Hughes had bought Barbara into contact with the Australian prime minister in 1916 when he visited England to stir support and make a sympathetic place for Australians in the minds of the British Cabinet. He was a vigorous, cantankerous, and eccentric man, 'a prince of story tellers and a master of nonsense'.[3] He had a lot in common with Barbara and, though there is no record of their appearance together in public before 1915, by the end of the war a friendship was well established. She was a literate defender of Australians and as ruthless and witty in arguments as he was, with one difference – she never bothered to use reason as her guide, a trait that amused him. 'I haven't a very good reputation myself when it comes to verbal disagreement but Barbara – she was bloody well impossible.'[4]

One of Barbara's collection of homilies included 'unreason is a woman's greatest weapon'. She may have thought it a particularly feminine strategy, but she used it on her women friends as well as on the opposite sex. Perhaps she thought it amusing to be able to get away with it. She certainly stopped short of using 'unreason' in her business dealings, and she twisted the saying 'Be good sweet maid and let who will be clever' to 'Be good sweet maid and let your Ma be clever' to keep Penelope in line.

Now in the first year of peacetime Billy Hughes recalled Henry Gullett from Palestine to accompany him to the Peace

Conference in Versailles – under the mistaken impression that Henry could speak French. Penelope could, but Henry was antipodean, if not antediluvian, in his approach to foreign languages. When his wife introduced him to a Parisian shoe manufacturer, also named Henry, the Frenchman referred to him as 'Enry' and he made an effort at French pronunciation, which came out as 'Hongry'. Enry and Hongry were typical representatives of their cultures and became firm friends.[5]

After the conference Hughes returned to London and was seen with Barbara at the theatre. Her friend Vance Palmer looked up one evening to see the prime minister seated by Barbara, who seemed 'a most imposing dowager'.[6]

In the interim between the signing of the peace treaty and the Hugheses' departure for Australia, Barbara got to know Dame Mary Hughes quite well. She had gone out of her way to make London a familiar and welcoming place to the wife of the prime minister. She held parties and invited leading people to meet the couple – carefully noting their verbal idiosyncrasies for future reference. She was with them at a party, surrounded by the British military establishment, when Billy Hughes once again commented on the inefficiency of the British High Command. He described an acquaintance as having 'hardly the brains of a cavalry officer'. General Haig, who was standing nearby, stepped forward and frostily reminded him that *he* was a cavalry man. The atonal voice droned on: 'As I said, he hadn't the brains of a cavalry officer ...'[7]

Vance Palmer met Barbara again at a party later that year, when they discussed literature once more. He guessed she had stopped writing, but whether it was because of the failure of *Human Toll* or because 'the harsh realities of the Bush that had nourished her talent were growing fainter in her mind', he did not know:

The life she was now leading – the life of country houses and great occasions – was not the sort she cared to write about, and I doubt whether she would have had the technique to cope with it. Anyone who reads the first page of 'Human Toll' will see how far her imaginative world was removed from Vanity Fair. But she still cared deeply for literature. I remember her talking to me enthusiastically in 1919 about Knut Hamsun's 'Hunger'; Knut Hamsun was then a new writer whom few people had read. And I remember her at the same gathering listening to an elderly Anglo-Australian journalist who, because she was a writer, thought she would be interested in discussing the fashionable novel of the day. She listened, staring at him in what could only be called an explosive silence, till suddenly she let go:

'Man! Why do you waste your brains by troubling to read such stuff? It's not for grown-up men and women; it's for poor creatures who take just what's given them by the girl at the library.'

The breath of vigor in her deep voice nearly blew him out of the window.[8]

The world was now turning into something Barbara began to lose step with. Whereas before she had moved with her times and in rhythm with the swell of Australia's expansion into the outer world and consolidation of its own image, now suddenly her step faltered. So, horribly consistent with her increasing age and the matriarchal air she had acquired, came a striking new note – a perceptively higher tone of querulous disapproval with the world around her.

By the end of the war Barbara had acquired a large collection of jewels which she wore with great relish, covering herself with many glittering bits and pieces when she felt she was on show. She had a long string of black pearls, a high choke collar of four or five layers of white pearls, a large diamond tiara, and a pair of enamel snake bracelets that wound round her wrists and dropped onto the back of her hands with rubies set in their heads. The pieces were important to her as symbols of her achievement and perhaps to replace the beauty that was fading. Her grandson describes her in one photograph as 'dressed in full battle order'. She was very protective of her jewels, and unpleasantly jealous. Mistrustful of reason she kept them in small packages in odd places around the house. She drew the curtains with her brooches pinned inside the lining, walked away and forgot them. On one of her trips to Australia she had sent an urgent telegram back to London ordering the household to arrest the butler. Shortly afterwards a mysterious but carefully wrapped brown parcel was found on the hall table, where she had left it. Walking through her mother's drawing-room Penelope often took off her shoes to avoid crunching over Barbara's necklaces spread out under the carpet.[9] Now Barbara was to acquire one that meant more to her than any other.

She had called the association she had formed to care for the soldiers the Australian Wanderers. The effects of her actions were to reach back past the boys at the front to their families and, most importantly for her, to the women who were their mothers. In 1916 she had written in 'Trooper Jim Tasman':

I know that these bereft mothers who take their sorrows silently, though what these stalwart sons were to them, who have little else, I, as a Bush woman know. Time and again I have watched for some comment on their sacrificing heroism, but I have never seen it. Maybe because it is not understood, for, happen what will to the European mother, she at least has companionship. 'Misery loves company.' The Bush mother must tell her grief to Nature, her only outlet.[10]

After the war the families and friends wrote to her to thank her. They sent letters and reminiscences. Some told stories the soldiers had told them, some let her know what had happened to this one or that. Many women wrote. From the parents and relatives of the eight thousand she had sheltered, she received one day a token of appreciation. They had all sent donations which, together, made a sum large enough to buy her a black opal, one of the first from Lightning Ridge. It was the size of a plum and she wore it with great pride.[11] The colours were dark and mystical and when it moved, a fault in the shape of a bird could be seen flashing in the stone. She wore it when she needed strength and reassurance, but she had a superstitious misgiving: the opal is regarded as an unlucky stone.

Sometimes the letters from the mothers of the men who had been killed were almost more than she could bear. She was still casting about for some belief to sustain her in the years immediately following the war. She dug deeper into Hindu religion to find some answer to the spectre of death that seemed to ride with her, blending the images of Rama, the

Hindu prince of truth and beauty, with the Christian figures of her youth to give her imagery the force she needed to describe the loss these bush women bore. 'In Rama. The Bush Mother' is not a lyric poem, and Barbara never acquired the technique to write good poetry, but it does show the mixture of contempt and helplessness she felt at such pointless sacrifice. Addressing the spectre of death, she mocks at his harvest of youth and advises him to take the mother too as a gesture of compassion, knowing that he will nevertheless find this a double victory:

With scythe agleam into thy garden go,
Where all the flower of youth doth bloom,
No shrift, nor sacrament, nor tomb;
But still their rich, ripe blood must flow,
Nor heed'st thou Rachel's cry of woe.
Oh, Death!

Now for thy vaunted chivalry,
While thy last sacrament she sips,
Close thou her lonely eyes and lips,
Take thou – oh, take her tenderly –
Then gloat upon thy victory.
Oh, Death![12]

Barbara had bought a small wooden figure representing a Chinese goddess of poetry. The woman is rounded and substantial, her flowing garments giving an impression of stateliness and some power. The expression is one of self-contained compassion. Perhaps it is an image of something Barbara would have liked for herself, but her search into other religions never replaced the early disillusionment of her days in the small chapels of outback Australia. She believed in prayer but seemed to turn to it only in a crisis, and she used religion as a prop to her existence, to inspire or dramatize, not as a substructure. Although the religious imagery of her writing was now filled with more exotic symbols, it was the exterior that still beguiled her, not the core. She seemed to get no comfort on her pilgrimage and to arrive not far from the place she had started from, but surrounded by more entrancing objects.

Henry Gullett had started final research and writing for his history of the campaign in Sinai and Palestine, and by the end of 1919 he had decided to move back to Australia. Penelope was pregnant with their second child and she had the opportunity of travelling back with W. M. Hughes and his wife at an early stage in her pregnancy. She and Henry wanted the family to grow up as Australians and felt it part of their duty to go back, despite the fact that Henry had good prospects in England and the flu epidemic, which had killed so many during that year, was only just now spluttering to its conclusion in Australia.

With this departure Barbara must have felt that an era of her life was ending. Penelope would have to stay with her young family, and she would be 12,000 miles away. Barbara, though comforted by her wealth, would be comforted by little else. Her son Alec and his bride planned to follow Penelope early in the new year, leaving only Robert, never to be considered a comfort under any circumstance.

Before they left, she took Alec and his wife, Lily, to the theatre. Many years later, Lily Frater described the evening:

Of course, me being young . . . Alec and Barbara and I went to dinner and to the theatre and I thought it was lovely – a little bit of fluff. To me it was the most exciting love scene. They came home and they criticized it. How awful it was, what a waste of money. I thought it was beautiful – this is just my version – and the next time we went to a play they thought it was marvellous. It was very high-brow. So you see the difference – gaps in the generations. But, oh! I did enjoy it – a love story. Just a bit of fluff but they were bored stiff, and I didn't know till we were going home.'

Although Barbara kept up with the stark force of modern literature, she found the new art 'puzzling', and the feeling of forced gaiety, unsettling and distasteful.[13] The enviable life, the life she wanted, changed from *comme il faut* to 'chic', and respect for elders disappeared with it. 'Today', she announced in an interview, 'people laugh and talk louder than ever before in the world's existence. No matter what your age or position, whatever air you take or whatever strata of society you mingle with you are shoved unceremoniously by youth.'[14]

Now in her sixties, Barbara wanted everything the old order had promised. She had the accoutrements, the money and the position, and suddenly the rules had changed. She wanted to play the *grande dame*, to be haughty and dictatorial. She wanted to use her position and enjoy it. Before the war she could have got away with it. Now it was too late. When Penelope's ship sailed back to Australia, with the prime minister and his wife aboard, she decided to follow.

Twenty

Early in 1920 in Melbourne Penelope gave birth to her second child, a daughter, Susan. The voyage to Australia had been an interesting one for her and the Hugheses. Billy Hughes had extended the friendship he had with Barbara and Henry Gullett to Penelope who had been an amusing companion for most of the time, except near the end, when tiredness after weeks at sea made them quarrel. All was soon forgiven, however, and at the birth of her daughter Hughes rode over on a white horse to bless the little girl in the 'name of the Commonwealth'.[1]

In an interview given to the Sydney magazine *Home* later that year, Barbara described Billy Hughes as a man of 'clear vision – a rare thing; a wonderful memory for facts and unfailing humour'.[2] He would need both when dealing with her. He was ruthless and persuasive but seemed to be brought to a complete standstill by Barbara and her daughter. With Barbara, the more perceptive his arguments became the more wildly fanciful she became until he could find no way around her; Penelope simply walked away. Neither one had any special reverence for his position, and they treated him with the same wry good humour with which he treated everybody else. They brought out a sense of playfulness in him. He could tease them and have fun without fear. If he went too far, they punished him or matched him, but neither was afraid.

By June 1920 Barbara was in Sydney meddling with the affairs of the Law Book Company. She regarded her appearances at the company's board meetings as high drama. She would arrive extravagantly dressed and immediately ruin the afternoon's proceedings by ordering a bottle of French champagne. At this time she was also casting about for future projects. She contemplated writing a series of children's stories and began work on some Australian cautionary tales for her grandchildren.[3]

At the end of the interview in *Home* she suddenly announced she was writing a new novel to be called *Wet Paint*, in which 'the bush, Sydney society, and London scenes will appear'. No trace of a manuscript for *Wet Paint* has ever been found. It is more likely to have been a flight of fancy rather than a fact. Perhaps she wanted to use what she had lived through to produce another novel. All her previous work had been based on her own experiences, but the failure of *Human Toll* and a nagging pressure to write something 'merrier' spoilt what may have been an attempt at another work.

By late August 1920 she was considering returning to England. She missed the galleries and the bustle of life. Penelope and the baby were well, and Alec and Lily Frater had had twins – another generation was beginning. But finally she decided to sell all her property overseas and then return to Australia permanently.

Another story was forming in her mind, prompted by the sight of familiar scenes in Sydney. On a trip visiting friends in the bush, she had risen before dawn to watch the countryside waking. She had walked far out to see the bird and animal life as it stirred into action. An emu rose stiffly from its nest, a dog barked at the hurdled sheep, lizards scrambled out of their shelters. Lying flat on her back she played childhood games with the crows – trying to dupe them into thinking her dead, then jumping to her feet to hurl sticks at them. The bush still fed her, despite her hatred of these terrible black birds. She had wandered on, seeing the wattle and dog orchids, wood violets and wild clematis from her childhood. Now that she was older and could choose, the bush seemed kinder to her.

She found two reasons to write again. She was struck by an imbalance in the appreciation of the European countryside as opposed to the Australian. In an article called 'Australian Spring' published in the *British–Australasian* in September 1921, Barbara stated the case for the Australian countryside. She thought it ridiculous that the bunch of flowers in her hands had been referred to as 'scentless' and the birds 'songless': 'I wonder if the man who wrote of them ... had a perpetual cold in his head and wool in his ears.'

The image of mother and child, in the bush as well as the city, surrounded her, and everything served to remind her of that basic comforting link. In both her interview and 'Australian Spring' she dwelled on the newborn and the maternal and remarked that the sight of Epstein's *Mother and Child*, emerging from what at first seemed a 'shapeless lump of rock' made a powerful impression on her.

Taking ship in December 1920 with Elisabeth Forster, a young friend from London and her children, Barbara was again suspended between two worlds: her new life as matriarch to an increasing number of grandchildren in her country of origin, and her old life, which was crumbling and changing into something she did not want. For a few weeks she was in a carefully controlled vacuum, but this time with an observer, John Forster, the young son of her travelling companion.

The ship was divided into three classes, first, second, and steerage. On most voyages the passenger list included members of the casts of plays touring the world, sportsmen, dancers and singers, and on this particular voyage John Forster remembered

a woman travelling on that ship who was a world-famous whistler, an Australian, and she was going to give concerts in England, and as part of the concert that night, I remember, she gave her sort of whistling performance. Not a bird imitation – straight out sort of whistling – almost Beethoven, probably Mozart or something. There were fancy dress games, there were race games, there was always something bloody going on. And the amount of *food* people ate was unbelievable.[4]

Barbara preferred to stay in her cabin with her friend, playing cards. John Forster had the impression Barbara didn't like many people and didn't want to waste her time meeting new ones.

Between two and four in the afternoon, when his younger sister, Morag, had a rest, the small boy was put in a cabin under the care of his mother while she played bezique with Barbara. Out of the list of card games Barbara could play, piquet, ecarté, whist, she preferred bezique with its two-pack sequence of marriages and royal marriages. While the two women played cards, Barbara gave the boy her jewel box to explore:

I can remember the case so well ... it had drawers. The front dropped down and you opened the drawers and there were the opals. I remember the sunburst (her collection of opals mounted as a tiara) because I remembered it when I saw it again in 1947. It was the sort of thing you put on a crown.

They sailed through the Red Sea and, despite the heat, Barbara remained in a black dress with a high choker, and a heliotrope scarf wound round her neck and thrown over her shoulder. To John Forster she seemed very tall and carried herself very straight.

Although Barbara had missed the galleries and social life of England, she had not changed into a European. Though impressed by pomp and grandeur she loathed pretence and arrogance, especially if it were not her own. She had quarrelled with Nellie Melba and now both women 'cordially detested and vigorously maligned the other'.[5] She spoke slightingly of other women's hauteur, though she relished moments when she could use it herself. She liked, she said, people in high places who were unostentatious and worked hard – a rare combination.

On arrival in England, Barbara contacted her usual circle of friends, including Lord Headley, who Barbara had continued to see since their first meeting in Hyde Park at the beginning of the war. He was now a widower. His wife Teresa had died in 1919. He owned an estate which was in disrepair, in Ireland, and was now attempting to maintain himself as he believed a gentleman should, on an engineer's salary. As a consequence he was broke. He proposed to Barbara, whom he had found a witty and amusing companion for many years and who must have looked like an ideal solution to his problems. For Barbara, with her heart in neither Australia nor England, marriage to a baron would mean better credentials in England than she had

had before, and the companionship of a man she had known for ten years. It seemed the right choice.

Their marriage was set for February 1921. None of Barbara's own family could be there in so short a time, and that in itself made the ceremony unreal, and divorced in its way from the rest of her life.

At sixty-six George Allanson-Winn, the Baron Headley, was two years older than Barbara and, so it would seem on paper, a very suitable match. The photographs of the pair show what appears to be a robust attractive man with a very old and quite unattractive woman. She had little time to choose her clothes and her fashionable tricorn gave her the look of a sailor facing into a strong headwind. She wore her opals slung low on a chain of pearls, partly covered by a sable, and she carried with her a bunch of wattle tied with a small net bow. This 'mimosa', as it was described in a newspaper article, was a token of balance against the dark stone, in memory, she said, of her association with the Australian troops, but it was also a touch-stone with Australia, for now she was more separated from it than she had ever been before.

Her friends the Kinnairds came down from Scotland to be with her. As usual they were there when she needed support. It is indicative of their care and her regard for them that she had only Lord Headley's sons and members of the Kinnaird family at the wedding.

The wedding was hastily arranged, and Lord Headley was known to be short of money. The gossip-mongers were delighted. Barbara arrived at the Registry in a closed, horse-drawn carriage and under-stated her age by a full decade. Articles appeared under the title 'Wedding Surprise', and Barbara was referred to as a rich Australian bride with literary tastes, 'whose age was given as 53'.

Outside the Marylebone Registry they paused for the inevitable press shots. The couple emerged from the building side by side, with Lord Headley smiling broadly and Barbara bowing her head toward him, pressing her lips together and carefully watching the newspapermen. In the general bustle Lord Headley forgot his suitcases and an umbrella he had brought with him and he had to send a taxi back to collect them. After the reception at Claridges, Lord Headley moved into Barbara's house in Connaught Square.

In an article in the *Daily Sketch* titled 'Peer's Romance, Lord Headley Married to Wealthy Widow ... Mohammedan Bridegroom Leaves Suitcases at Registry', Barbara described their plans for the next ten days:

'And the first part of our honeymoon will be spent in the unromantic city of Birmingham, because Lord Headley – I mean (smiling) my husband – has to lecture there to-morrow night,' said Lady Headley. 'And after that I have no doubt we shall have a little holiday somewhere nice.'

It was doubtful whether the 'little holiday somewhere nice' ever eventuated. She spent a thrilling few days listening to his plans to tunnel under the Goodwin Sands for buried treasure hidden in the holds of sunken ships. It was hardly an auspicious start.

A day later, under the heading 'An All-Round Irishman', an article described vividly the man Barbara had married:

Lord Headley's quiet espousal of an Australian wife yesterday brings again into the newslight the Goodwin Sands salvage scheme which his lordship has just proposed. His sensational conversion to Islam occurred, it will be recalled, at the height of the suffrage movement. A great adventurer, Lord Headley was reported to have perished in Mashonaland nearly thirty years ago, but turned up in the House of Lords some two and a half years after his alleged demise.

The famous Irish peer is best known in some circles, not for his engineering genius, religion, possessions, or adventures, but for his standard writings on the 'noble art of self-defence'.[6]

A photograph taken of Barbara at this time is strikingly different from any other. It shows a smiling apple-cheeked matron with grey hair and a dazed look that must have been meant to pass for pleasant. It looks as if the effort almost cost her her sanity. It has none of the bright penetrating stare of the photograph of 1916. It was a bad portrait and it offended her, but it was done by a fashionable photographer in London and was part of a general lean toward 'merriment' and sweetness that had crept into her life. She would have been much better to acknowledge the sheer strength in her character, rather than burying it under this burden of saccharine, but outside influences now weighed heavily against her.

Barbara's fear of her own lack of femininity drew her toward overtly masculine men who resolved all doubts. Her contradictory nature had led her to campaign against suffrage, while her whole life had been a triumph of survival for a woman of no means in a dangerous, masculine and brutal society. George Allanson-Wynn had also campaigned against suffrage, but with no contradictory impulses. He believed implicitly that women should not vote by divine intention; no make-up, no independence, no freedom and no vote. How shocked he must have been as the twenties wore on and first the ankles and then the knees went skimming past him in a swirl of brightly coloured beads followed by a faint haze of tobacco. His wife was shocked also, but for different reasons.

They found it difficult to meet on any terms. He was a fit and practical man, scrupulously polite, but given to 'imaginative calculations' which were partly to blame for his comparative poverty.[7] The suitcases left behind at the wedding were the suitcases out of which he had been living. He dressed well, spoke well, looked well, and charmed people, but his society was almost exclusively masculine, and not only masculine but elderly masculine and British. He expected to have a wife who would restore him to the place his family had occupied before. He wished once more to be a peer of some importance. He certainly expected to hold the purse strings.

Despite their long friendship, Barbara and Lord Headley soon found living together as man and wife a strain. After the wedding, Barbara cemented her claim by hurrying down to her engraver to have the lion guardant with cross gules and eagles with wings inverted put on all the lesser pieces of silver, but the continuing drain on her finances, caused by the upkeep of Lord Headley's estate in Ireland, began to annoy her.

One of the soldiers staying in Barbara's house during the war had been Martin Boyd, the young cousin of Charles Chomley, editor of the *British–Australasian*. After the war he had returned briefly to Australia, but by 1921 Barbara had offered to let him stay at Connaught Square. He was talented and poor, a twenty-eight-year-old Australian from a good family in Melbourne. She became his patroness, giving him money and clothes, and the time and space he needed to write. He installed a gramophone in his room and played endless tunes to himself while he worked. In 1921 he was developing his skills as an author and he turned his attention to Barbara and her marriage. While he had to make guesses he could not verify on matters such as Barbara's background and financial affairs, and the appearance of Lord Headley's property in Ireland, Aghadoe House, he drew a sketch of the marriage between Barbara and Lord Headley at a time when he would have been staying in her house in London for long periods in between his newspaper assignments in Europe. In the novel *Brangane*, published in 1926, Aghadoe House appears as Walton and Lord Headley under the name 'Lord Pulborough'. An excerpt describing him reads:

Whatever the occupation of the moment, his fancy would seize on it and roam to amazing distances. When he drank his tea, he might regard the shape of his cup, and consider if it would float. He would enlarge on the idea and wonder if it were possible to sail a boat the size of the teacup, and how much he would be prepared to stake on the possibility. Supposing he were offered ten thousand, no, say twenty thousand pounds to cross the Channel in an enlarged tea-cup, would he accept the offer? It was possible that the handle would render the cup unfloatable. But, assuming that it would float, how could it be directed without bows or stern? One might have two little propellers fixed underneath, but would that, by changing the outward appearance of the cup, contravene the terms of the wager? If he crossed the Channel and won the twenty thousand pounds, how would he spend it?

His fancy flew further.

If he were walking down Piccadilly he might wonder how many times the width of Piccadilly would go round Walton Park. Or how many times the total area of Piccadilly would go into Walton, and what would be the value of Walton if land there were worth as much as in Piccadilly.

He would awaken from such reverie to give polite replies to Brangane, who, as far as he was concerned, was the unsatisfactory result of an imaginative calculation.[8]

Barbara's reaction to Lord Headley's financial problems was given greater edge when she realized how absolutely business-like his intentions in this marriage were. He had bestowed the family seat of Aghadoe on her at the time of her marriage, a beautiful old place in Ireland, overlooking the lakes of Killarney, but it was mortgaged and decaying and its upkeep weighed heavily on her. It was as if he had made the marriage to preserve himself and his estate, but for an exchange that became untenable. A marriage in the proper sense was unthinkable to him – he would have preferred to cross the Channel in an enlarged teacup.

Barbara began to notice his personal habits around the house and to comment on them:

She was sitting over the drawing-room fire when her husband entered. The very sight of him irritated her. Brangane liked people with vigour, people like Daphne with whom one could exchange hearty blows. Pulborough gave her no sense of resistance. He had something of the quality of a mouse. Even his hair and his eyebrows were mouse-coloured. He was like a very tall mouse.

'Do you mind if I smoke?' he asked.

'Yes I do,' said Brangane sharply.

He gave a slight bow and sat down.

'The servants complain that you are untidy,' she said, opening the attack.

'Are you accustomed to accepting the judgement of your servants?' he asked quietly.

'I am not accustomed to an untidy house.'

'Naturally.' He spoke with no trace of feeling.

Brangane's annoyance increased. Why couldn't the man answer back instead of sitting there, so indifferent and self-possessed?

'By the way, I'd be glad if you would use the other bathroom,' she added, hoping to sting him to retort.

'Certainly,' said Lord Pulborough, and opened an evening paper.[9]

He smoked in the bathroom and wafted about the house treating her with icy politeness. By August 1921 he was talking of a marriage breakdown and shortly after sent a letter to his solicitors, advising them of his intention to separate from his wife.

Barbara had put the word 'Desormais' on the fly-leaf of *Human Toll*, as if to exorcise that part of her life that was enclosed within it. From now on ... But in September 1921 she published another short story in the *British–Australasian* which shows clearly how little she had lost the old feeling of blight.

With breathtaking clarity she describes her own greed and ambition, giving her heroine the same qualities she had had as a girl. Caroline Bell sneers at sentiment and tawdriness; she walks past rows of tombstones in a small country graveyard, her lip curling with contempt as she reads 'with cool scorn the maudlin epitaphs'. She loathes her sisters' homeliness, and openly sizes up her only admirer for the pros and cons of his suit. He had money but his manner was awkward and churlish. He had strength and compassion, but he lived 'twenty-three miles from any town'. In the end, she goes away to consider her dilemma, leaving him with little encouragement. 'Well, I can just as readily see myself turn into a bush hermit as you into a townsman.' After a restless two weeks, she decides for him and returns – to find him strolling along Manly Pier, engaged to her sister. 'But all her lifetime she had never once got just what she wanted, and she had made up her mind that she never would.'

Barbara had taken snippets of Alex Frater for her male character, Robert Ingall, and she had revealed herself in a savagely clear light, but throughout the story there is grimness and a presentiment of doom. It was published, under the florid title 'Her Bush Sweetheart' and was never given much critical attention, but it reveals much more of her than some of her early work. If she wrote this during her third marriage, perhaps it was prompted by the knowledge that she had repeated her original mistake.

The similarities between Lord Headley and her first husband were many. He liked gambling, he was appealing, and, as an engineer, his mind was occupied with practical ways to 'fix' things, as Alex's had been. He was an athlete with an easy flow of movement, just as Alex had been a confident and assured horseman. Both were used to manly things, manly ways and manly pursuits, and neither finished anything precisely or thoroughly as Dr Baynton had taught Barbara to do.

The marriage continued to deteriorate and finally Lord Headley left the house, but not before one last contretemps.

In Muslim circles Lord Headley was known as Saifurrahman Shaikh Rahmatillah Farooq, a name which gave rise to much merriment in the local press. The *Daily News* decided it was unnecessary for him to dig in the Goodwin Sands for treasure, he should simply murmur 'Open Sesame' and the sands would eject their golden wealth with the 'vim of a catapult'. But it was no laughing matter to him. He was president of the British Muslim Society and as such was offered the vacant throne of Albania, going begging for want of survivors. Barbara's phoenix, having settled on a rickety branch of the English aristocracy, now took off in full flight. Thrones, processions, regalia. The sense of unreality, and a feeling of increasing transitoriness that she detested would vanish completely under the weight of a crown. But, to her astonishment, he turned it down.

After checking the statistics, Lord Headley had found that the rate of survival for Albanian royalty was unsatisfactorily low. As a consolation prize, 'certain notables of that country' offered Barbara a fine blue sapphire brooch, and asked her to tell them frankly if she liked it. Her grandson, H. B. Gullett, in a foreword to an Australian reprint of *Bush Studies* described her reaction:

She replied with fullsome thanks but added that since they asked her, she in fact already possessed a blue sapphire brooch. She would therefore, prefer a brown sapphire. Brown sapphires are generally more prized than blue ones. But eventually a magnificent stone was duly found, set, and presented.

By October, after a harrowing few months of legal proceedings, Barbara was ill with the strain, but she refused to give in to Lord Headley's demand for a divorce and a financial settlement. Early in 1923 she suddenly cabled Penelope to come to her immediately.

Arriving at Connaught Square, exhausted and fraught, having travelled half-way across the world on her own, Penelope sat down at the end of the long dining table and leant forward wearily.

'*Take* your elbows *off* the table', came instantly from the other end.[10] The old fire was still there, but unsteady itself now.

The wrangling continued. He wanted his family's memorial ring back. She wouldn't give it – couldn't find it. Where were the letters she had sent him? Finally the ring was found and the letters returned, but only after months of dispute that stretched into years, during which Lord Headley suddenly took off on a pilgrimage to Mecca. Finally on 10 June 1924 they both signed a judicial deed of separation. All allegations were withdrawn and she was alone again.

She tried to wipe it away and proceed with her life, as she had before. When asked about the reason for her divorce she said: 'Dis*gust*ing old man – he used my hairbrushes.'[11]

A photograph taken about this time shows Barbara in a long black beaded dress with her black pearls, a choker, and a tiara on her grey, and obviously difficult-to-handle, hair. The expression of simpering sweetness has given way to a weary guardedness, the direct straight smile of 1916 darkened by suspicion.

Twenty-one

Not long after the divorce, Barbara headed back to Australia, and though the relentless details of the divorce had wounded her, she was by no means down. A short while after her arrival she visited Rose Scott, now an old woman. An article on the encounter proves once again how much her friends were, without exception, intelligent and good people:

No stranger contrast can be imagined, and no two women more utterly unlike than Miss Scott and Mrs. Baynton, the former with her serene nature and uplifted ideals in human goodness – which no ingratitude from those whom she often helped without any return but carping criticism – could shake, the latter, with at that time, very little belief in anything when in one of her moods that resembled a mind enveloped in dark and sombre clouds.

These lifted for she had her sun-shiny days, her wit and charm without anything that the world counts as good looks, made Mrs. Baynton an inimitable comparison.

It was one of her whims to ring up before going to Miss Scott to ask her 'If I come to lunch will you give me some dry pumpkin?' There are seasons when dry pumpkin – a very different edible from the wet mashy pulpy kind – is as hard to get from the most obliging Chinaman as coal in flooded creek. In the midst of many plans for the welfare of humanity Miss Scott, whose charming home was near Edgecliff, had to soak her mind in the pursuit of dry pumpkin or some other sudden fancy hurled through the phone at the last moment.

Mrs. Baynton was one of the most brilliant conversationalists one ever met. And but for that caustic touch, her knowledge of literature, French and English, her acquaintance with famous men and women on both sides of the equator – she knew London as well as she knew Brisbane and Sydney – made her a delightful encyclopedia.

Amongst the men who were once perhaps more loudly lauded than today, was Count Tolstoy. To Mrs. Baynton, he was anathema. To Miss Rose Scott he was a benign philanthropist, her 'dear Tolstoy'.

On the last occasion I met Mrs. Baynton in Miss Scott's drawing-room – the nearest approach to a salon that Sydney knew – Tolstoy's name was the climax of argument in which the lady of the house in her gentle voice asked.

'But what will posterity do about the great humanitarian?'

'Serve him up on toast, and give him to the devil to munch,' was the reply.[1]

Despite this singlemindedness, or maybe because of it, Barbara was an asset to have anywhere, but like any great asset, she took a little looking after. A more colourful and vivid picture of Barbara emerges from this period as many more witnesses survive.

Her daughter had settled in Melbourne, which was still the centre of government, with her husband and they planned to build a house next door to suit Barbara. It would have a large garden and access through a paved courtyard to their own. Jean Ferguson, the daughter of Stewart Ferguson, the family doctor, remembered the house. 'I can see her house very vaguely – almost like a dream. It was not a light house – a dark house. I think she was probably lonely, but I don't know. There were awful fashions. I see her in a rather floppy dress and the wisps, always the wisps of hair. I think she was fond of Henry but it was difficult – a mother-in-law next door. Even in the best of circumstances.'[2]

Henry Gullett had been appointed minister for immigration on his return from England and was a director of the Australian War Museum, which he had helped to start with C. E. W. Bean. However, after a prolonged argument with Billy Hughes over immigration Henry resigned his position, and the day after received an imperious cablegram from Northcliffe in London, 'Desire you assist me Times', offering him the editorship.[3] But Henry Gullett wanted to help in the postwar reconstruction and to let his children grow up as Australians, so he joined the staff of the *Herald* in Melbourne and resolved to re-enter politics as a critic of the prime minister. He was cheerfully irreverent to the imposing figure next door.

Barbara settled comfortably into her house and began to enjoy herself buying furniture and decorations for it. As Henry had been in the Middle East, and Dr Baynton had been fond of rugs, she bought several and invited him to give his opinion. She asked if they were genuine. The only true way to tell, he said, was to turn the hose on them and if the colours ran they were fake. A carpet was dragged out, the hose found and, as the grass turned from green to red to dark brown, the answer was obvious. But she forgave him – he had found a chauffeur for her. An ex-soldier who had driven Prime Minister Billy Hughes around on his pro-conscription tour of Australia in 1916, Wallace was fit and stoic, an ideal 'minder' and a man with a medium-length fuse. She ordered a bright red Daimler for him to drive.[4]

She liked company and would often drift next door to her daughter, arriving sometimes when a card game was in progress. Unable to join she would sit on the sidelines and comment – and she was capable of bringing anything to an abrupt halt.

In the years leading up to its publication in 1926, Martin Boyd was writing *Brangane*, with Barbara's comments fresh in his mind:

Daphne brought a Mr. Basset-Burne, a coy and elderly bachelor, to play bridge. He chatted gaily throughout the evening. Brangane lost three rubbers.

'I suppose you ladies wonder why I have never married,' he said, leading the wrong card.

Brangane looked at him sweetly.

'Is it by any chance because you're a eunuch?'[5]

Barbara's visits to the Gulletts must have been a strain at times and yet the atmosphere remained quite light, mostly because of the temperament of her son-in-law. Henry Gullett walked into his house one day and noticed a familiar hat hanging on a peg in the hall. Clapping it onto his head he marched into the drawing-room doing a fine imitation of

Barbara's imperious voice, a ringing crescendo announcing, 'I've been robbed, I've been *robbed!*' Barbara's frozen person and his wife's horrified gaze met him. There was a pause, and then Barbara laughed, and they laughed and the moment passed.

She wrote stories for the children, tapping them out on her typewriter and testing them on Vera, the Gulletts' nanny. She read straight from the type and it must have been important to her. Her vision was poor, and she did not waste her 'good eyes' on rubbish. They were cautionary tales, grim and satirical, silly, sometimes lightheartedly violent – a mixture of Edward Lear and Aesop. A hen and her chicks, Silly Sally the duck. A fox, rat and snake, a crow and 'other symbols of human unpleasantness and folly'.[6] They produced a delicious mixture of fear and delight at bedtime. She never published them and at her death Penelope burnt them.

There was dawning in Barbara a fear that her work was superficial and that it would not last. She would certainly not end her life with a collection of farmyard fables. She had faith in *Bush Studies* and she kept a copy near her and patted it occasionally. She re-read the stories often and referred to the book affectionately as 'The Studs'. Though she seldom talked about the stories, they were a continuous source of satisfaction. She knew as far as she could tell that they were good, but she needed reassurance. Her grandson, H. B. Gullett, remembers her putting the book down with 'a wide cynical smile as if to say, "you may not care for it, but it's not bad – do better yourself" '.

She was also working on a serial, which harked back to her first marriage, for an Australian newspaper. Two undated episodes of the story, 'Drought Driven', have been found in Alec Frater's scrapbook. The detail is crisp and has an immediacy that suggests the memories lived with her from day to day. Perhaps these were written at an earlier time, but it seems unlikely she would have left work unpublished for so long, especially a serial. The bush was still in her, though she could command it to approach or recede through Wallace, her chauffeur. She recalled now the first time she had seen a snake, she had made a mental pact with it – don't you hurt me and I won't hurt you, and how as a young mother she had found

Alec playing with a large black snake under the house. She had backed away quite calmly and later the child had come inside unhurt. She remembered the smell of the acrid water in drought time, and how it tasted 'going down', and the sun as it set in a great red ball that seemed to be 'sucking the hearts' out of the dying animals.

In her Melbourne house, Barbara began to espouse household duties, adding her own touch of majesty to the proceedings. She used the huge copper in the laundry for cooking jam and sent Wallace down to stir it occasionally. Wallace politely put on his driving goggles and gloves and plodded down the garden path. She dragooned the whole household into these efforts, and the effects were picturesque: Wallace in full uniform, with his goggles misted over by steam, and Penelope sitting patiently stirring the goo, smoking a cigarette in a long holder. During one of these tours of duty Penelope's engage-ment ring slid from her finger into the mess and was never seen again.

After these invigorating rituals, she would offer the bottled results to her friends, and, despite her son-in-law's warnings, some were foolish enough to eat it. She herself was often the unconscious victim, not that she ever admitted it. Penelope found her sitting by the window, crunching through crackly things on her toast. On closer inspection she saw the glacé remains of a wasp in Barbara's jam. 'Ah, yes,' said her mother, 'I'd forgotten I'd put nuts in it.'[7]

At night she and her 'faithful coloured maid'[8] drifted over the courtyard to collect a bottle of champagne from her daughter's cellar. Barbara had always had Aboriginal com-panions in the bush and one of her most beautiful female characters, the only woman who ever escapes an ill fate, is Woona, the young black girl in *Human Toll*, who outwits and enchants her older husband and fades in and out of the white woman's life like the quick bright spirit she herself will never be.

Barbara was good and generous to most people in her household and many incidents have been recorded involving the white women around her, but there is only one reference to her Aboriginal maid. It is possible this girl was part of the notorious system that took black children from their parents early and sent them as domestics to city women. Barbara had become close to black Australians during her early married life when she was so isolated. Alec's nickname 'Lappy' was supposed to be taken from an Aboriginal word and it is likely her first children were delivered with the help of black women. Now she began to refer to herself as 'Agda'. She told her grand-daughter it was Aboriginal for 'wise one', but it may also have been a mispronunciation of 'grandma' by her grandson, H. B. Gullett.

Younger people were drawn to her as a sort of mythical figure. Intimidated by her image, they treated her with the wariness of a child sitting down at a long table, with the faint image of Miss Haversham at the other end. Harking back to her days in the outback millinery, she tied huge bows on her granddaughter Susan's hair, and the child staggered off barely upright under the weight of these sophisticated decorations. Occasionally next door at the Gulletts they heard her playing the piano, 'wild and weird'.[9]

On nights when the Gullett family were away, she kept her grandson's dog for him. 'Jock' was a big black part-kelpie, whose loyalty to the little boy was legend. He waited outside school for him and had occasionally been savage in his defence. Vera the Nanny was next door in the Gulletts' house one night when she heard a terrible sound coming from Barbara's house. Rushing over, she found Barbara on the floor with her hand to her face and blood pouring out. The dog had leapt at her when she moved to pick up a large telephone directory, and bitten through her top lip:

She was very brave and I telephoned the doctor, Stewart Ferguson, and he came immediately. Later he asked me to stay with her and to hold her hand while he sewed up the wound. Just iodine was used – it must have been terribly painful. She was so very brave, and later when she felt better she sent me some antique Wedgwood dishes.[10]

Some time later, when the dog bit Barbara's granddaughter Susan, it was immediately put down.

Throughout her years in Melbourne, Barbara had trouble keeping the domestic status quo. The humiliation of the divorce had set a seal on her. The only man she had loved had died and there was now no hope for another. Her friends were dwindling, and there were few people now who had known her for much of her life. In 1925 Rose Scott, who had been her mentor and sometime mediator, died, and it was left to Barbara's family to provide her with challenges and to keep her company. She had always known how to put people at ease, but the force of her personality now was slightly unnerving. Her surroundings and the fact that age had given her face a sort of monumental look made meetings with the Lady Headley a daunting experience. She herself was in a slow anguish, which made her sensitive to slight and overly possessive of her friends. She would take violent umbrage at something one of the household had done and tear into the people around her with horrifying clarity and incisiveness. Then, when the sharp edges faded in her mind, her real vulnerability showed and she confused the issue by being genuinely contrite. Worse, and more confusing, was her appalling remorse. Penelope would have to explain the tears away and Henry smooth things over with 'fair words and the whisky decanter'.[11] Barbara looked around the house and gave small objects away as tokens of her apology.

In autumn 1925 she received a letter from Ethel Turner. From the tone of the letter it would seem Barbara had a friend who knew her well and was not afraid of her, a combination she needed in these years. Barbara was obviously planning a trip to the bush again.

April 4th 1925

Dear Barbara,

You asked me for my favourite poem. Here at last is one of them, Wordsworth's 'The World' – so I give it to you as a treasure of great price. And *as* a medicine! While you are among those lovely gum trees you are to read it and forget all about shares and cares and jewels &– &– &–. And you are to lie on the grass & shut your eyes & let have a hearing that 'core' of yours that I have always felt is a thing of great power & originality and wildness. A deck chair in the middle of the ocean in front of you would also serve. And then you are to write some more of those verses that are in you asking to be born...

> *The world is too much with us; late and soon,*
> *Getting and spending, we lay waste our powers:*
> *Little we see in Nature that is ours;*
> *We have given our hearts away, a sordid boon!*
> *This sea that bares her bosom to the moon;*
> *The winds that will be howling at all hours,*
> *And are up-gathered now like sleeping flowers;*
> *For this, for everything, we are out of tune;*
>
> *It moves us not. – Great God! I'd rather be*
> *A Pagan suckled in a creed outworn;*
> *So might I, standing on this pleasant lea,*
> *Have glimpses that would make me less forlorn;*
> *Have sight of Proteus rising from the sea;*
> *Or hear old Triton blow his wreathèd horn.* [12]

It may have taken an old friend to sense that something had changed in Barbara. In urging her to write, Ethel Turner was perhaps trying to force her to commit whatever feelings she had to paper, as she had done before. Writing poetry had always been a cathartic experience, even if her work had been uneven and now seems dated and ponderous.

After Rose Scott's death Barbara ceased all attempts at journalism and seems to have lost interest in all causes, except for the care and protection of children. She supported a fund for waifs and strays and carefully explained the plight of these children to Alec's daughter Alexandra.

She visited her son Alec in Sydney, staying in a hotel or occasionally with the family. She used this house as her own and entertained her friends there if she felt like it. She had long conversations with Steele Rudd about his financial predicament and they talked about life in the bush. On one of Rudd's visits Alec's wife Lily froze outside the door, horrified at the language. Barbara was discussing travel in the outback and had used the word 'buggy' several times, which the young woman had misheard. [13]

159

By now, Barbara's elaborate taste in food and years of good cooks had brought to light an ailment in that in leaner times may never have shown itself. She had a weak liver and this, and the indigestion caused by rich food, made her carry a little box of peppermint-flavoured soda mints. Otherwise she ignored her complaint and continued to drink champagne, though the effects overcame her more quickly than before.

Barbara was bored in Melbourne. She no longer wrote articles or studied the outside world around her. She needed stimulation and she picked on her household, creating small melodramas to while away the hours. She particularly enjoyed tormenting Wallace, the chauffeur. The car she had bought had a sliding glass that divided the driver from the occupant sitting behind him in a cabin with a roof high enough to stand up in. There was a console with knobs to enable her to speak to the driver, but Barbara had trouble mastering this small piece of equipment. At times when she thought he was driving too fast, or too slow, she pressed a button and asked him what he was doing. Having pushed the listen button to talk and the talk button to listen she got no response and promptly pushed them both. Wallace had an ear piece that protruded from the front of the car and into his ear. The effect of both buttons being pushed simultaneously produced a piercing shriek an inch away from his cranium. And just for good measure she slid the door back and prodded him in the neck with her umbrella. On one of these occasions he put his foot on the accelerator and revved the pace up so that Barbara was thrown from side to side as he raced up hill and down dale, swerving to a halt in a spray of gravel outside her house. She got out, adjusted her dress, glanced at her shoes and swept off, turning to say: 'Thank you Wallace. You drove quite well. For once.'[14]

She was variable and moody about the house and often seemed to be lonely. In 1928 when her daughter moved away to Canberra, where the new national parliament was established, she was even more alone, but not without resources. She held parties; her grandchildren visited her; and she invited people to stay. She tried to resolve the hazy images of religion in her mind, moving toward a greater sense of the spirit than she had ever given time to before. She had the Bishop of Willochra to stay. She talked openly about religion. She told Vera she believed in the power of prayer, and her spiteful moods alternated with just enough kindness to keep friends and people about the house who were good and thorough in their work, though the road was rocky on occasion.

As she grew older, she hated the cold and tried to spend every winter away. Vera could not remember seeing her in winter clothes and in these later years she took several trips back to England, dodging the seasons. She bought and sold furniture each way, changing and rearranging her possessions and enjoying the drama of the auctions she held in her house. She relied absolutely on Mrs Dawes, the housekeeper, Wallace, and Stewart Ferguson to look after her.

As usual when life was moving at a slow crawl, she decided to rearrange her house. In April 1928 she held an auction and sold practically everything she had of value. She planned to go to England and use the proceeds to travel around the antique shops and auction houses buying up a whole houseful of interesting pieces to bring back to Australia. It was one way of spending the time, and she decided she would take Alec's daughter Alexandra with her as child protégée, and show her the world. Alexandra and her twin sister Joan had come to stay, but Joan had been sick and gone home, leaving Alexandra to stay with Barbara for several months. Barbara loved having young children to visit and she would have enjoyed the companionship, playing grandmother to a child she could dress up and spoil and show off to her friends. She did not bother to ask Lily Frater for permission to sail away with the child, but considering it would mean four or five months away from the family Lily refused to allow it. There is no record of Barbara's reaction to this, except a receipt for overpayment of her fare to England – approximately the amount of a child's ticket.

Barbara had brought back a painting of herself from her trip to London the previous year. It was done by a popular British portraitist, Anton Anrooy, and shows a matron with grey hair and a sweet smile. Barbara loathed it. Not only because the artist had been unable to paint her opals, but because she thought it unflattering. A portrait of her daughter by Tom

Roberts and another of herself by British watercolourist Spencer Pryse were also dismissed and lost forever through her habit of banishing paintings to the cellar.

And so in 1928 she sailed away to another English summer, of which no record remains. She must have led her usual life in London, contacted her friends at the *British–Australasian*, and bought a new houseful of furniture.

For her to redecorate her house in Melbourne, which she had stripped practically bare, meant a great deal of bustle around London, but her health was not good and, despite the beauty of the spring, at seventy-one she felt her age. There were gaps now that she could not fill: many of her English friends had died, and the attitude of the *British–Australasian*, crisp and respectful in her heyday, had become slightly mocking. She returned to Melbourne.

She came back thankfully, happy to be in the clear bright air of the Victorian spring, away from the growing sense of economic doom that was spreading through Europe.

The great distances she had covered so often in ocean liners were now being skipped over by light aircraft, reducing the mental distance from one end of the globe to another to a handspan. What had taken weeks of enforced idleness was now a matter of days. But Barbara, who had spent so many months at sea travelling between England and Australia, was never to fly; it was the beginning of the end for the great ocean liners and the absolute end of the life she had known. Australians Charles Kingsford-Smith and Charles Ulm were making a name in the air and slowly the vast inland spaces began to be covered by a network of aeroplanes bringing medical and postal services to the bush. Women were part of this surge into the skies and it was a daring and inspiring enterprise. Barbara had a circle of friends in London who entertained and encouraged women flyers, but she found these socialites brittle and full of artifice and abandoned her contacts with them early.

As the summer of 1928–9 passed, she planned another trip. The garden was in full bloom. Walking down the path to inspect her flowers she fell heavily. Wallace carried her inside, but her hip was badly broken and despite careful nursing she did not heal.

In an attempt to lighten her spirits Billy Hughes sent her a letter, which he ended with a lighthearted prayer for her recovery to 'God the Father, and God the Son – and so say all of us, and God save the King'.[15] Penelope came to nurse her, but on 28 May 1929 Barbara died from pneumonia.

She had spent the last few weeks of her life writing intricate and contradictory wills, with only one clear sentence that can never be misunderstood. She wished to be buried next to Thomas Baynton. The addition on his tombstone was to read simply 'and his wife Barbara'.

Penelope went through her mother's house and threw out things she thought of no importance. A bundle of children's stories called *The Book of the Bush* was burnt. The house was full of antique rugs, china, paintings and furniture from England, which after a final sale, filtered out and around Melbourne.

Two years later, at the height of the Depression, one of Sarah Glover's daughters found Alex Frater in a hostel for old men, and stayed with him through his final illness until he died, intestate.

Elizabeth's grave on a hill at Murrurundi became neglected and finally forgotten; the wings of the monumental angel on the neighbouring grave of Ben Hall have been battered off by loveless tourists. In the following years John Lawrence, the carpenter, died. Lord Headley married an heiress.

Alec kept his scrapbook and faithfully tended his family until his death. Penelope continued all things bright and beautiful. Robert lived to enlist in the Second World War, grossly understating his age, and with a heavily dyed moustache. He joined the Merchant Marine, being years too old for any other service, and when his ship was sunk in the bitter North Sea he surfed to the Scottish shore on a piece of broken decking. Barbara did not mention him in her will.

Barbara lived in the rooms of the house of my childhood, as clearly as anyone I can remember. On one side, under glass on the dressing table, was a picture of a substantial matron, slightly awkward, posing for the camera in a heavily beaded dress. On the other side of the room was a photograph in a small frame of a young woman with a high, stiff collar and a bright proud smile. In a painted wooden chest was Barbara's lorgnette and a string of cloisoné beads my mother had bitten flat as a child. In the swirl of leaves and strange birds on the pattern of her curtains, and the odd pieces of information about her life – the warnings against laziness, improvidence, stupidity – 'nothing more catching than boredom, nothing more dangerous than a fool' – I always saw the older woman. Walking on her carpets, looking through glass at her porcelain, she was forever a matriarch to me, a woman of property. But when I read *Bush Studies*, the girl in the small portrait came into focus. Later the two became one. Perhaps everyone comes slowly to their beginnings and knows the place for the first time. I was born years after Barbara's death and had no chance to hear anything other than the echoes.

Notes

Chapter One (pp. 1–5)

All page references to Barbara Baynton's work are taken from a collection of Barbara Baynton's work published under the title *Portable Australian Authors: Barbara Baynton*, edited by Sally Krimmer and Alan Lawson, Queensland University Press, St Lucia, Qld, 1980.

1. Lord Salisbury to Barbara Baynton, commenting on Australian troops in the Boer War, included in the version of 'Trooper Jim Tasman' published in England in the *British–Australasian*, 21 July 1916, and subsequently omitted from the edition of *Bush Studies* republished under the title *Cobbers* by Duckworth & Co., London, 1917.
2. Barbara Baynton, 'Trooper Jim Tasman', *Portable Australian Authors*, p. 92.
3. Charles Dickens's description of an Australian wharfside scene in 1852, from R. M. Younger, *Australia! Australia!*, Rigby, Adelaide, 1975, pp. 236–7.
4. Historical Notes, *Journal of the Quirindi District Historical Society*, vol. 2, no. 6, p. 95.
5. Edith Potter, *The Scone I Remember*, Scone and Upper Hunter Historical Society, Scone, NSW, 1981, p. 90.
6. ibid., p. 151.
7. Susan Hackforth-Jones, Penelope Baynton's daughter, granddaughter of Barbara Baynton, interview, 8 June 1982.
8. Mrs Nancy Gray, of the Scone Historical Society. For this and other information regarding the Lawrences I am indebted to Mrs Gray.
9. James Ewart's birth certificate.

Chapter Two (pp. 6–10)

1. Registration of arrival of Robert Kilpatrick, carpenter, on the

Crescent, 11 February 1840, Archives of New South Wales.

2   Penelope Ranger, daughter of Sarah Glover and Alex Frater, interview, 27 June 1982.

3   Ken Frater, son of Sarah Glover and Alex Frater, interview, 19 June 1982.

4   Barbara Baynton, 'Indignity of Domestic Service', *Portable Australian Authors*, p. 321.

5   Barbara Baynton, 'Her Bush Sweetheart', ibid., p. 109.

6   Susan Hackforth-Jones, interview, 8 June 1982, plus probable autobiographical reference in 'Drought Driven', an undated serial by Barbara Baynton.

7   Penelope Ranger, interview.

8   Edith Potter, *The Scone I Remember*, p. 22.

9   Barbara Baynton, 'A Dreamer', *Portable Australian Authors*, p. 7.

10   Ken Frater, interview.

Chapter Three (pp. 11–15)

1   Barbara Baynton, *Human Toll,* in *Portable Australian Authors*, p. 174.

2   ibid., p. 175.

3   Mrs Nancy Gray, Scone Historical Society, 1982.

4   Barbara Baynton, 'Toohey's Party', *Portable Australian Authors*, p. 99.

5   Barbara Baynton, *Human Toll*, p. 186.

6   ibid., p. 185.

7   Barbara Baynton, 'Billy Skywonkie', *Portable Australian Authors*, p. 47. Incident reconstructed from information collected by D. B. Jamieson in Narrabri, NSW, March 1955, from his great-aunt Mary Isobel Faulkner (née Frater), sister of Alex Frater and a pupil of Barbara's at Merrylong.

8   Barbara Baynton, 'Billy Skywonkie', p. 46.

9   ibid., p. 58.

10   ibid., p. 60.

11   Information on Frater Family from Frater family Bible, in possession of D. B. Jamieson.

Chapter Four (pp. 16–19)

1   Frater Family Bible, fly-leaf, family tree.

2   Interview of M. I. Faulkner by D. B. Jamieson, March 1955.

3   ibid.
4   Frater Family Bible.
5   D. B. Jamieson, interview, 16 April 1983.
6   Interview, Faulkner/Jamieson.
7   D. B. Jamieson, interview, 16 April 1983.
8   Frater Family Bible.
9   Interview, Faulkner/Jamieson.
10 Extract from 'Diary of John Allan – A Trip to Trinkey Station about 1860', Historical Notes, *Journal of Quirindi District Historical Society*, vol. 11, no. 1.
11 Family entries, Births, Deaths and Marriages, Hunter Valley District, 1843–4.
12 Interview, Faulkner/Jamieson.
13 Illuminated address in the possession of Don Frater.
14 Interview, Faulkner/Jamieson.
15 ibid.

Chapter Five (pp. 20–3)
1   Interview of M. I. Faulkner by D. B. Jamieson, March 1955.
2   Barbara Baynton, 'Bush Church', *Portable Australian Authors*, p. 68.
3   Interview, Faulkner/Jamieson.
4   D. B. Jamieson, interview, 16 April 1983.
5   Interview, Faulkner/Jamieson.
6   ibid.
7   Ken Frater, interview, 19 June 1982.
8   Don Frater, son of Alex Frater and Sarah Glover, interview, 19 June 1982.
9   Interview, Faulkner/Jamieson.
10 Interview of Fanny Ritter (illegitimate daughter of John Frater and a pupil of Barbara Baynton at Merrylong) by D. B. Jamieson.
11 Interview, Faulkner/Jamieson.
12 Interview, Ritter/Jamieson.
13 Interview, Faulkner/Jamieson.

Chapter Six (pp. 24–9)
1   Interview of M. I. Faulkner by D. B. Jamieson, March 1955.
2   Barbara Baynton, 'The Chosen Vessel', *Portable Australian Authors*, p. 81. This story was used to reconstruct Barbara's

early married life.
3 Ken Frater, interview, 22 June 1982.
4 D. Jamieson, interview, 16 April 1983.
5 Alec Frater's birth certificate, 3 November 1881.
6 Ken Frater, interview.
7 Penelope Ranger, daughter of Alex Frater and Sarah Glover, interview, 27 June 1982.
8 D. B. Jamieson, interviews, 4 June and 16 July 1982.
9 ibid.
10 Barbara Baynton, 'Bush Church', 'Jyne' is based on Mrs Lennard. D. B. Jamieson, interviews.
11 D. B. Jamieson, interviews.
12 Penelope Ranger, interview, 27 June 1982.
13 ibid.

Chapter Seven (pp. 30–8)
1 Divorce papers, *Frater* v. *Frater*, 1888, Supreme Court of New South Wales.
2 ibid.
3 D. B. Jamieson, interview, 16 July 1982.
4 ibid.
5 Divorce papers, *Frater* v. *Frater*, 1888.
6 ibid.
7 D. B. Jamieson, interview.
8 Penelope Ranger, interview, 27 June 1982.

Chapter Eight (pp. 39–43)
1 Divorce papers, *Frater* v. *Frater*, 1888, Supreme Court of New South Wales.
2 Lily Frater, wife of Alec Frater, interview, 30 August 1982.
3 D. B. Jamieson, interview, 16 July 1982.
4 Interview of Fanny Ritter by D. B. Jamieson.
5 Divorce papers, *Frater* v. *Frater*, 1888.
6 Marriage certificate of Thomas Baynton and Barbara Frater, Sydney, 1890.
7 Susan Hackforth-Jones, interview, 1 April 1983.

Chapter Nine (pp. 44–50)
1 Penelope Ranger, interview, 27 June 1982.

2 ibid.
3 Penelope Ranger, interview; divorce papers, *Frater* v. *Frater*, 1888, Supreme Court of New South Wales.
4 Penelope Ranger, interview.
5 ibid.
6 ibid.
7 Ken Frater, interview, 19 June 1982.
8 Penelope Ranger, interview.
9 Ken Frater, interview.

Chapter Ten (pp. 51–5)
1 Marriage certificate, Thomas Baynton and Barbara Frater.
2 Barbara Baynton, 'Indignity of Domestic Service', *Portable Australian Authors*, p. 322.
3 Susan Hackforth-Jones, interview, 1 April 1983.
4 ibid.
5 ibid.
6 ibid.

Chapter Eleven (pp. 56–68)
1 Susan Hackforth-Jones, interview, 1 April 1983.
2 D. B. Jamieson, interview, 16 April 1983.
3 Interview of M. I. Faulkner by D. B. Jamieson, March 1955.
4 C. J. Maguire, An original reaction from art: Analysis of the criticism of A. G. Stephens on the Red Page of the *Bulletin*, 1894–1906, unpublished PhD thesis, Australian National University, 1972.
5 Kylie Tennant, 'Miles Franklin: Feminist whose men were men', *Sydney Morning Herald*, 23 July 1974.
6 Barbara Baynton, 'The Tramp', later retitled 'The Chosen Vessel' when it was published in *Bush Studies* and *Cobbers*. After its initial publication in the *Bulletin*, 12 December 1896, Barbara Baynton restored the section concerning Peter Hennessey and his vision and re-edited the story. *Portable Australian Authors*, p. 83.
7 Barbara Baynton, 'Scrammy 'And', *Portable Australian Authors*, p. 28.
8 Letter from Barbara Baynton to A. G. Stephens in the Hayes collection, Fryer Library, University of Queensland.

9 A. G. Stephens, quoted in C. J. Maguire, An original reaction from art.
10 Barbara Baynton, 'Bush Church', *Portable Australian Authors*, p. 77.
11 Henry Parkes, *Australian Views of England: Eleven Letters Written in the Years 1861 and 1862*, Macmillan, London and Cambridge, 1869, pp. 17–18.
12 Letter from Alfred Deakin to Rose Scott, November 1903. Scott Family Papers, Mitchell Library.
13 Letter from Stella M. Franklin to Rose Scott, 2 December 1904. Miscellaneous correspondence of Rose Scott, Mitchell Library.
14 Untitled newspaper clipping.
15 Barbara Baynton, 'B.B. to the *Bulletin*', *Portable Australian Authors*, p. 315.
16 ibid.

Chapter Twelve (pp. 69–76)

1 Barbara Baynton, 'A Dreamer', *Portable Australian Authors*, p. 5.
2 Barbara Baynton, unpublished poem held in the Hayes Collection, Fryer Library, University of Queensland.
3 Unidentified newspaper article.
4 Barbara Baynton, 'To-Morrow', *Portable Australian Authors*, p. 306.
5 Lily Frater, interview, 30 August 1982.
6 Barbara Baynton, *Human Toll,* in *Portable Australian Authors*, p. 205.
7 Lily Frater, interview.
8 Rudyard Kipling, 'The Ballad of the King's Jest'.
9 A. G. Stephens, quoted in C. J. Maguire, An original reaction from art.
10 ibid.

Chapter Thirteen (pp. 77–86)

1 Unidentified newspaper article in a scrapbook kept by Alec Frater.
2 Barbara Baynton to Nellie Melba; letter first published in a biography of Melba by Agnes Murphy in 1909, and subsequently in *Portable*, p. 317.
3 H. B. Gullett, interview, 20 August 1983.

4 Unidentified newspaper article in Alec Frater's scrapbook.
5 Vance Palmer, 'Writers I Remember. 1. Barbara Baynton', *Australia Overland*, January 1958.
6 Barbara Baynton, 'Address to the Writers' Union', *Sydney Morning Herald*, 6 July 1911.
7 *Daily Mail*, London, 20 January 1903. Duckworth's publicity handout. A. G. Stephens's scrapbook, Mitchell Library.
8 London *Academy and Literature*, 24 January 1903, Duckworth's publicity handout.
9 London *Literary World*, 13 February 1903, Duckworth's publicity handout.
10 Melbourne *Age*, 24 January 1903, Duckworth's publicity handout.
11 Adelaide *Advertiser*, 17 January 1903, Duckworth's publicity handout.
12 Glasgow *Herald*, 22 January 1903, Duckworth's publicity handout.
13 A. G. Stephens, Red Page essay, 'One Realist and Another', *Bulletin*. Alec Frater's scrapbook.
14 A. G. Stephens, Red Page essay, 'The Bush', *Bulletin*, Alec Frater's scrapbook.
15 *Darling Downs Gazette*, Duckworth's publicity handout.
16 Barbara Baynton to A. G. Stephens, Hayes Collection, Fryer Library, University of Queensland.
17 Undated unidentified article, 'The Author of "Bush Studies." A visit to Brisbane', Alec Frater's scrapbook.
18 Barbara Baynton to A. G. Stephens, September 1903, Hayes Collection, Fryer Library, University of Queensland.
19 Lawson's Auction Catalogue, The Magormadine, 12 September 1904.
20 Lily Frater, interview, 5 August 1983.

Chapter Fourteen (pp. 87–94)
1 Unidentified article, 'The Author of "Bush Studies." A visit to Brisbane', Alec Frater's scrapbook.
2 Barbara Baynton, *Human Toll*, in *Portable Australian Authors*, p. 220.
3 Barbara Baynton, unpublished poem, 'Mateless', in A. G. Stephens's Papers, Hayes Collection, Fryer Library, University of Queensland.

4   Lawson's Auction Catalogue, The Magormadine, 12 September 1904.
5   Dr Baynton's will, 12 November 1895.
6   Lily Frater, interview, 30 August 1982.
7   Susan Hackforth-Jones, interview, 8 June 1982.
8   *Sydney Morning Herald*, 4 October 1904.

Chapter Fifteen (pp. 95–102)
1   H. B. Gullett, interview, 3 January 1988.
2   ibid.
3   *Sunday Times*, undated article in Alec Frater's scrapbook.
4   Vincent Brown Postcard, review of *Human Toll*, Alec Frater's scrapbook.
5   Barbara Baynton to Nellie Melba, *Portable Australian Authors*, p. 317.

Chapter Sixteen (pp. 103–8)
1   *Sydney Morning Herald*, 23 July 1904.
2   ibid., May 1908.
3   Barbara Baynton, 'Indignity of Domestic Service', *Portable Australian Authors*, p. 318.
4   Lily Frater, interview, 5 August 1983.
5   Barbara Baynton, 'Indignity of Domestic Service', p. 318.
6   'Martin Mills' (Martin Boyd), *Brangane*, Constable and Co., London, 1926. Interview with H. B. Gullett, 11 November 1983, on Barbara Baynton's reaction to the publication of Martin Boyd's novel in 1926, which he had heard from his mother, Penelope Baynton.
7   Susan Hackforth-Jones, interview, 8 June 1982.

Chapter Seventeen (pp. 109–16)
1   Susan Hackforth-Jones, interview, 1 April 1983.
2   ibid., and H. B. Gullett, interview, 11 November 1983.
3   'England and the Australian Writer – Barbara Baynton's Experience', *Sydney Morning Herald*, 6 July 1911.
4   Susan Hackforth-Jones and H. B. Gullett, interviews.
5   Barbara Baynton, 'To-Morrow's Song', first published in the *British–Australasian*, 24 July 1913; *Portable Australian Authors,* p. 307.

6 Lily Frater, interview, 30 August 1982.
7 Charles Barrett, 'Barbara Baynton's Books. An Appreciation'. *Sydney Morning Herald*, 26 July 1929. The article quotes a letter Barbara Baynton wrote to a naturalist in Melbourne.
8 Susan Hackforth-Jones, interview.
9 H. B. Gullett, interview.
10 ibid.

Chapter Eighteen (pp. 117–31)
1 H. B. Gullett, interview, 11 November 1983.
2 ibid.
3 'An Acquisition', *Pall Mall Gazette*, 11 May 1921, Alec Frater's scrapbook.
4 'An All-round Irishman', *London Daily Chronicle*, 12 February 1921, Alec Frater's scrapbook.
5 H. B. Gullett, interview.
6 Vance Palmer, 'Writers I Remember'.
7 ibid.
8 Lily Frater, interview, 30 August 1982.
9 Barbara Baynton, 'The Australian Soldier. An Appreciation and a Tribute', *British–Australasian*, 19 November 1918; *Portable Australian Authors*, p. 323.
10 F. R. Hocking, honorary secretary of the Gallipoli Legion of Anzacs, interview.
11 Law Book Co. records.
12 Barbara Baynton, 'Trooper Jim Tasman', *Portable Australian Authors*, p. 92.
13 *Osteralia*, souvenir magazine of the AIF troops on board RMS *Osterley*, G. Harmsworth & Co., London, 1917.
14 Barbara Baynton, 'The Australian Soldier', p. 325.
15 Susan Hackforth-Jones, interview, 1 April 1983.
16 Lily Frater, interview.
17 Barbara Baynton, 'Trooper Jim Tasman', p. 94.
18 Barbara Baynton, 'The Australian Soldier', p. 324.
19 Barbara Baynton, 'Rare Banqueters', *British–Australasian*, September 1918; *Portable Australian Authors*, p. 309.

Chapter Nineteen (pp. 132–9)
1 Lily Frater, interview, 30 August 1982.

2   H. B. Gullett, interview, 2 July 1986.
3   H. B. Gullett, 'Memoir of Barbara Baynton' in *Bush Studies*, Angus & Robertson, Sydney, 1965.
4   ibid.
5   H. B. Gullett, interview.
6   Vance Palmer, 'Writers I Remember'.
7   H. B. Gullett, interview.
8   Vance Palmer, 'Writers I Remember'.
9   Susan Hackforth-Jones, interview, 1 April 1983.
10 Barbara Baynton, 'Trooper Jim Tasman', *Portable Australian Authors*, p. 92.
11 'Lord Headley Married', London *Daily Mirror*, 12 February 1921, Alec Frater's scrapbook.
12 Barbara Baynton, 'In Rama. The Bush Mother', first published in the *British–Australasian*, September 1919; *Portable Australian Authors*, p. 309.
13 Barbara Baynton, interview in *Home* magazine, 1920; *Portable Australian Authors*, p. 326.
14 Unidentified article.

Chapter Twenty (pp. 140–51)

1   Susan Hackforth-Jones, interview, 1 April 1983.
2   Barbara Baynton, interview in *Home* magazine, 1920; *Portable Australian Authors*, p. 326.
3   Vera Amos, interview, 1 June 1981.
4   John Forster, interview, 4 April 1983.
5   H. B. Gullett, 'Memoir of Barbara Baynton'.
6   'An All-round Irishman', London *Daily Chronicle*, 12 February 1921.
7   Martin Boyd, 'Brangane', p. 142.
8   ibid., p. 143.
9   ibid., pp. 139–40.
10 Susan Hackforth-Jones, interview.
11 ibid.

Chapter Twenty-one (pp. 152–64)

1   Unidentified article.
2   Jean Thurlow (née Ferguson), interview, 22 September 1981.
3   Susan Hackforth-Jones, interview, 1 April 1983.

4 ibid.
5 Martin Boyd, *Brangane*, p. 121.
6 H. B. Gullett, 'Memoir of Barbara Baynton'.
7 Susan Hackforth-Jones, interview.
8 Lily Frater, interview, 1982.
9 Susan Hackforth-Jones, interview.
10 Vera Amos, interview, 1 June 1981.
11 H. B. Gullett, 'Memoir of Barbara Baynton'.
12 Letter from Ethel Turner to Barbara Baynton, Lady Barbara Headley, Papers 1907–38, National Library of Australia.
13 Lily Frater, interview, 30 August 1982.
14 Susan Hackforth-Jones, interview.
15 Barbara Wilson (née Frater), interview, 2 November 1987.